JAMES W. SIRE

DISCIPLESHIP OF THE MIND

Learning to Love God in
the Ways We Think

INTERVARSITY PRESS
DOWNERS GROVE, ILLINOIS 60515

InterVarsity Press is the book-publishing division of InterVarsity Christian Fellowship, a student movement active on campus at hundreds of universities, colleges and schools of nursing. For information about local and regional activities, write Public Relations Dept., InterVarsity Christian Fellowship, 6400 Schroeder Rd., P.O. Box 7895, Madison, WI 53707-7895.

Distributed in Canada through InterVarsity Press, 860 Denison St., Unit 3, Markham, Ontario L3R 4H1, Canada.

All Scripture quotations, unless otherwise indicated, are from the Holy Bible, New International Version. Copyright © 1973, 1978, International Bible Society. Used by permission of Zondervan Bible Publishers.

The haiku "The sea darkens" on p. 172 is taken from Japanese Literature: An Introduction for Western Readers, edited by Donald Keene, and used by permission of Grove Press, New York, N.Y.

The haikus "On a bare branch" (p. 170) and "A cuckoo—" (p. 172) are from Matsuo Basho, published by Kodansha International Ltd. © 1982 Reprinted by permission. All rights reserved.

Cover illustration: Robert Roper

ISBN 0-87784-985-4

Printed in the United States of America

Library of Congress Cataloging-in-Publication Data
Sire, James W.
    Discipleship of the mind: learning to love God in the ways we
    think/James W. Sire.
        p.   cm.
    Includes bibliographical references.
    ISNB 0-87784-985-4
    1. Christianity—Philosophy.   2. Christianity and culture.
3. Education (Christian theology)   4. Evangelicalism.
5. Bibliography—Best books—Christianity.   6. Civilization,
Modern—20th century.   I. Title.
    BR100.S517   1990
201—dc20   89-48575
                                                       CIP

16   15   14   13   12   11   10   9   8   7   6   5   4   3   2   1
99   98   97   96   95   94   93   92   91   90

*To university students
who want to love God
with all they are—
heart, mind and strength*

Acknowledgments

I would like to thank the many students, faculty and friends who have heard me speak so long and intently on the subject of this book. Their patience has been remarkable and their feedback vital.

Special thanks go to Brian J. Walsh and J. Richard Middleton for updating their "A Bibliography We Can't Live Without" published earlier in their own book *The Transforming Vision* (InterVarsity Press, 1984). I thought it then the best guide to the best that is being thought and said by and for Christians. It is even better now.

Finally, to my editor, James Hoover, goes my gratitude for his toughness. He has kept me from many faux pas and downright errors. What of those remain are my responsibility.

The fear of the LORD is the beginning of wisdom, and the knowledge of the Holy One is understanding.

Proverbs 9:10

Have this mind among yourselves, which you have in Christ Jesus.

The Apostle Paul to the Philippians[1]

We have the mind of Christ.

The Apostle Paul to the Corinthians[2]

The Christian mind—a mind trained, informed, equipped to handle data of secular controversy within a framework of reference which is constructed of Christian presuppositions. The Christian mind is the prerequisite of Christian thinking. And Christian thinking is the prerequisite of Christian action.

Harry Blamires[3]

Chapter 1
The Christian Mind:
The Beginning
of Wisdom

I came alive on a ranch on the rim of the Nebraska Sand Hills. I grew up like Wordsworth who

> . . . bounded o'er the mountains, by the sides
> Of the deep rivers, and the lonely streams,
> Wherever nature led.[4]

I loved riding horses and hiking in the hills. I loved the little stream that flowed past our house. I began to learn the cattle business, for my father and grandfather who lived with us raised purebred Herefords. I was sensuously awake, immersed in experience. But my mind was a blank. I never had a philosophic thought in my life.

Annie Dillard in *An American Childhood* puts it this way:

> Living you stand under a waterfall. . . . The hard water pelts your

skull, bangs in bits on your shoulders and arms. The strong water dashes down beside you and you feel it along your calves and thighs rising roughly back up, up to the rolling surface, full of bubbles that slide up your skin and break on you at full speed.[5]
Indeed life begins like that. Sheer experience. Then sometime during childhood, usually not all at once, we wake up. We don't just take in sensations. We wake up to ourselves and others. We become conscious that we are separate from the rest of the cosmos. You become aware that you are you. I find out I am I.

For me this occurred sometime just before the seventh grade. We had moved from the country to a small town in northern Nebraska. I had begun attending the village church just across the street from our house. And I had become a Christian. My best friend was the son of a missionary on furlough from Africa. We spent a lot of time together, discussing all kinds of things, some of them religious.

One day the same question occurred to both of us, and we couldn't puzzle out an answer: If God is all powerful, why would he ask people to believe in him? Why didn't he make them believe in him?

Predestination and free will—there it was, one of the all-time philosophic stumpers. Our minds were turned on. Counsel was sought from my friend's father. The answer was, as I recall, a rather good one. But the damage—some would say—was done. My mind would never turn off again. Experience alone—standing thoughtless under the waterfall—was no longer enough. I would have to know why—why the waterfall, why me, why anybody, why anything at all. And, since I was a Christian and knew that God was always involved in some way, the answers would have to be Christian.

Now, nearly fifty years later, my mind on that point has not changed. God has got to be involved in every thought—the conscious or unconscious backdrop to all consciousness, all nonconsciousness. But how? What does it mean to have a Christian mind? On that my mind has changed over the years.

I have long wanted to put down in orderly fashion my best thoughts on just what a Christian mind is, how it comes into formation, how it can be shaped and honed and made to reflect more and more the mind of Christ. And I have begun to do this over the past twenty years, often lecturing on what I labeled the Christian world view. It has only been recently, however, that I have taken seriously what many others have known all along.

The Christian mind does not begin with a world view, not even the Christian world view. It begins with an attitude. Granted that attitude is rooted in the Christian world view, it is nonetheless first of all an attitude. As an adolescent I would never have asked about predestination and free will if I had not already been impressed by God's awesome power. My question came from a primitive recognition that God is God and I am not.

The Christian Mind as an Attitude toward God

God is God and I am not. Put in its simplest form that is the basic orientation of every Christian mind—child, adolescent or adult, simple or profound. The Bible puts it much more elegantly, of course.

The fear of the LORD is the beginning of knowledge,
but fools despise wisdom and discipline. (Prov 1:7)

Variations on this text appear twice more in Proverbs and once in the Psalms (Prov 9:10; 15:33; Ps 111:10). But perhaps Job, when he quotes this proverb, says it best. Struggling to understand his undeserved suffering, Job asks his friends who have come to comfort him:

Where then does wisdom come from?
Where does understanding dwell?
It is hidden from the eyes of every living thing,
concealed even from the birds of the air.
Destruction and Death say,
"Only a rumor of it has reached our ears."
God understands the way to it

And he alone knows where it dwells,
for he views the ends of the earth
    and sees everything under the heavens. . . .
And he said to man,
    "The fear of the Lord—that is wisdom,
    and to shun evil is understanding." (Job 28:20-24, 28)

Each of these proverbial sayings begins with the same phrase: *the fear of the Lord*. If one is to be wise or have knowledge or good understanding, then the fear of the Lord must come first.

What is this fear? Our English word is inadequate for the concept, for it suggests being scared of the dark or of some imagined denizen of the night or of an armed robber who holds us at gunpoint. These are intense but passing emotions. The *fear of the Lord* is more sustained, more like *awe*. Yet *awe* doesn't suggest for most of us the strange numinous quality that should at least be the background of our attitude.

We can get a better sense from Wordsworth's boyhood experience when one evening he stole a boat and rowed out on a mountain lake.[6]

It was an act of stealth
And troubled pleasure, nor without the voice
Of mountain echoes did my boat move on.

Facing the shore, as one does when rowing out, he used as his reference point a craggy peak in front of him. As he rowed, suddenly from behind that first peak appeared a much higher peak hidden from view from the shore. With each stroke of the oars, the mountain rose higher, till it seemed to stride after him. Wordsworth quickly turned back to shore, remoored the boat,

And through the meadows homeward went, in grave
And serious mood; but after I had seen
That spectacle, for many days my brain
Worked with a dim and undetermined sense
Of unknown modes of being; o'er my thoughts

There hung a darkness, call it solitude
Or blank desertion.

That "serious mood," that "dim and undetermined sense of unknown modes of being," that "darkness," that sense that something is going on here and I don't know what it is, those moods when they persist over days, over our lives—that is what the *fear of the Lord* is like. It is predicated on a lot more than a mountain rising up on the horizon. It is predicated on God as God—Yahweh, the great I AM, HE WHO IS (Ex 3:14). We are all his creatures—finite, fallen. He is the infinite, the perfect. When we see where we stand in relation to him, we can only stand in awe.

Like Moses we are faced with the God who spoke out of the burning bush: "Do not come any closer. Take off your sandals, for the place where you are standing is holy ground." As God identified himself as "the God of your father, the God of Abraham, the God of Isaac and the God of Jacob," Moses "hid his face, because he was afraid to look at God" (Ex 3:5-6). Moses indeed knew his proper place: he stood in "a worshipping submission *(fear)* to the God of the covenant who has revealed Himself by name."[7]

Two of the basic texts mentioning the *fear of the Lord* as the beginning of wisdom also add a further dimension. The psalmist says, "all who follow his precepts have good understanding" (Ps 111:10); and Job says, "to shun evil is understanding" (Job 28:28). This brings out what is already implicit in the Hebrew concept of *wisdom*. Wisdom is more than intellectual knowledge. True, knowledge is involved (Prov 9:10), but the main matter is wisdom—the practical outworking of genuine knowledge. In Hebrew thought, "wisdom is the art of being successful, of forming the correct plan to gain the desired results."[8] That means that a truly Christian mind is not going to be the useless appendage that is often thought, a mind that engages in theological debate but never enters the realm of life as lived. Genuine Christian thought will result in obedience to God. Knowledge must lead to action. We will see more of how this works out in chapter six.

The main point here is that the Christian mind has a spiritual base. It begins with an attitude toward God. He is the source of all wisdom, all knowledge. What a contrast to René Descartes who founded his whole method on the one thing he took as indubitable, his own ego: "I think; therefore I am"! Quite the opposite is true. We are dependent on God as I AM and hence as our creator. We are *not* because we think; we think because we are—in fact, because we are like God.

The Christian Mind as an Attitude toward Ourselves

The flip side of the Christian mind is our attitude toward ourselves. This can be stated in one word: *humility.*

But what a word! We founder at every attempt to make it characteristic of our lives. But Jesus was humble, and in this as in many other things he is both our model and our pioneer.

> Have this mind among yourselves, which is yours in Christ Jesus, who, though he was in the form of God, did not count equality with God a thing to be grasped, but emptied himself, taking the form of a servant, being born in the likeness of men. And being found in human form he humbled himself and became obedient unto death, even the death on a cross. Therefore God has highly exalted him and bestowed on him a name which is above every name, that at the name of Jesus every knee should bow, in heaven and on earth and under the earth, and every tongue confess that Jesus Christ is Lord, to the glory of God the Father. (Phil 2:5-11 RSV)

Jesus left what was rightfully his—his place in glory. He became everything we are as human beings, even bearing in our place the burden of our sins. Jesus is humble. And—dare we say it? Of course, we do. God is humble. Jesus is the kind of God God is.[9] In his infinite knowledge and wisdom, in his absolute moral perfection, in the total awesomeness of his power, he has the character of humility. "God so loved the world," we so often say. But only if he were also humble could his love be expressed as it was in sending himself in his Son to take on the form of his own creation and to pay the just penalty for our sin.

It is indeed Jesus' humility that led to his exaltation. As Paul says, "Therefore God has highly exalted him." There is a fragment from the Greek philosopher Heraclitus which has always fascinated me as a commentary on this notion: "The way up and down is one and the same."[10] The way to glory for Jesus was by the cross. The way to glory for us is by following Jesus in a similar humility. John Howard Yoder writes, "Only at one point, only on one subject—but then consistently, universally—is Jesus our example: in his cross."[11]

"We have the mind of Christ," says Paul (1 Cor 2:16) as he concludes another long passage about the central message of the Christian faith. What he means is not that we somehow have the physical mind of Christ or even his supernatural mind in some mystical form, but that we have the mentality of Jesus as he lived a life that led to the cross. In the much misunderstood second chapter of 1 Corinthians, Paul is not putting down intelligence or true wisdom, as so many have thought. He is instead saying that God's foolishness, the foolishness of the cross, is wiser than the wisdom of the world. And we who are Christians have that mind. We live in the shadow of the cross of Christ, shouldering our own cross, bearing the burdens of one another, standing counter to the world and suffering for it. To have the mind of Christ is no mystical experience granted to those Christians who are especially holy. It is simply the attitude of humility toward oneself and service to God and others.[12]

A Recipe for Humility?

But how can we be humble? We fail so miserably when we consciously try. When we examine ourselves to see just how humble we are, we become proud of our humility and undercut our efforts. Are we forever trapped in a paradox? Well, I'm no expert in humility, but I don't think so. Humility turns out to be not a product of direct effort but a byproduct of the fear of the Lord. If I keep my eyes on God and keep my mind off myself, humility will follow. Humility is then a byproduct of our spiritual orientation—how we understand our relationship with God.

The apostle Peter puts it this way:

Clothe yourselves with humility toward one another, because,

"God opposes the proud

but gives grace to the humble."

Humble yourselves, therefore, under God's mighty hand, that he may lift you up in due time. (1 Pet 5:5-6)

The apostle James agrees: "Humble yourselves before the Lord, and he will lift you up" (Jas 4:10). For both Peter and James humility is not produced by comparing oneself to others or by self-abasement, saying to oneself, "Poor me! I'm just a worm." Humility is produced by seeing oneself in the light of who God is. Then, too, both Peter and James see Christian humility producing the same results for Jesus' followers as it did for Jesus. God raised Jesus from the dead and brought him into glory. We too will be raised and brought to glory. Glory and humility are not so far apart after all!

Humility also applies to our theology. We believe as Christians that God is omniscient and that we, as much as we know, as much as God has told us in his Word, are finite and fallible in our knowledge. We should, therefore, keep our own developing views of everything— God, human beings, nature, ourselves—in perspective. On any of these we could be wrong.

There is an old proverb worth our reflection:

When someone is honestly 55% right, that's very good and there's no use wrangling. And if someone is 60% right, it's wonderful, it's great luck, and let him thank God. But what's to be said about 75% right? Wise people say this is suspicious. Well, and what about 100% right? Whoever says he's 100% right is a fanatic, a thug, and the worst kind of rascal.[15]

In our more lucid moments we all acknowledge this. But when we come to our most cherished beliefs, those we hold most dearly and tenaciously, we forget we are prone to error. We strike out against anyone who questions our fundamental beliefs or wishes to state his or hers somewhat differently. We suddenly become proud that we know what our critic does not. We lose whatever humility we had and lock ourselves in a tidy room where we become bishop and king of our own point land.

Or we become locked in the tidy confines of our social enclave. That is what happened to the religious leaders of Jesus' day. The Shema was indelibly engraved on their psyche: "Hear, O Israel: The LORD our God, the LORD is one" (Deut 6:4). They thought they knew what it meant. So when Jesus said, "I know him [God] because I am from him and he sent me" (Jn 7:28-29), they refused to believe him. After all, they reasoned, God is one. There could not be a person so intimately attached to God that he could practically proclaim divinity. For the unity of God must be preserved. Here before them was one who was challenging their most fundamental conviction about the nature of God. If they are right about God, then Jesus can't be. What were they to do?

We know what they did. John tells us that "they picked up stones to stone him, but Jesus hid himself, slipping away from the temple grounds" (Jn 8:59).

How can we prevent the same sort of intellectual pride in ourselves? I think it can best be countered by recognizing just what it is we are often claiming. We are claiming to know God perfectly. How can we do that? He is infinite. We are finite. He can reveal anything he wants to anyone he chooses. But we can still misunderstand his revelation. When I become so sure that I have it right that I stand against all comers, I come close to standing against God himself, making him conform to the box in which my concept of him has put him. But God is bigger than my box or anyone's box. "I am who I am," said God to Moses. This difficult-to-translate Hebrew phrase may well include the idea "I will be what I will be" or "I will be whoever I show myself to be." In any case, it is the death of any perfect human theology of God.

I like the lines of Alfred, Lord Tennyson:

Our little systems have their day;
They have their day and cease to be;
They are but broken lights of thee,
And thou, O Lord, art more than they.[14]

Lesslie Newbigin echoes this in prose:

We can never claim that either our understanding or our action is absolutely right. We have no way of proving that we are right. That kind of proof belongs only at the end.[15]

And John Stott comments,

Systematic theology is certainly a legitimate and even necessary academic discipline, but God did not choose to reveal himself in systematic form, and all systems are exposed to the same temptation, namely to trim God's revelation to fit our system instead of adapting our system to accommodate his revelation.[16]

There is, of course, a balance. We need to be confident enough in our beliefs to act but not so dogmatic about them that we do not allow them to come under scrutiny. We should recognize the inadequacy of our own understanding and the sinfulness of many of our actions and yet commit ourselves to kingdom actions with a vision of the city of God always in our sights. Jesus has gone before us through death.

We should, then, put these twin attitudes of *fear* and *humility* into the perspective of the end times. What is worth preserving in our lives will be like the wealth of the nations that Isaiah envisions the kings of the surrounding nations bringing into Zion, the city of David (Is 60:1-14), and that the book of Revelation sees being brought into the heavenly city at the end of time (20:24-27). But there will be much dross that will be left behind.

The Christian Mind in Motion

The Christian mind is always in both formation and reformation. For any given person or community of believers it is never a finished product. On the one hand, it is being hewed from a Christian's growing grasp of Scripture in the context of a recalcitrant culture. On the other hand, it is being reformed through experience with God and his people and a growing understanding of what Scripture really teaches.

In *formation* it seeks to operate under the values of the kingdom of God. This requires persistent Bible study, not just as we engage in private devotions each day, but also as we intentionally address Scripture with the tough questions of life. What is God really like? How can we know him and know that we know him? How should we then live? We shall see how those questions are answered in the ensuing chapters.

Moreover, in formation the Christian mind requires regular reading of books written from a Christian perspective. Others have been down these paths before us; their trailblazing can make the way easier for us. For a guide to what I think are the best and most basic books, see the appendix.

Finally, in formation the Christian mind requires persistent obedience to God, practicing what we learn from studying Scripture and reading Christian books. This is what Os Guinness calls "the responsibility of knowledge."[17] If we think we know yet do not do, then from a purely biblical sense we do not really know. We will look at this theme in chapter six.

In *reformation* the Christian mind is self-critical. Regardless of how long we have been Christians, we must be critical of our past understanding. Doubt itself can be the midpoint between error and truth. Most of all, a Christian mind is always open to new understanding from Scripture. Each time we read the Bible we should take the attitude that the last time we read the passages we are reading today we might have misunderstood them, at least in part. There might be much more for us this time. This will keep us open to the possibility of growth in knowledge.

In reformation the Christian mind is always being informed by our experience. We act on the truth by obeying it, that is, by conforming our lives to the way we think things are. When the results are what we expect (or better, which is often the case), our beliefs are confirmed. When the results in our lives belie our understanding, we have to rethink our views. This becomes an endless process this side of glory.

Finally, in both formation and reformation the Christian mind is other-critical: It constantly seeks to understand and weigh the value of its environment. This requires various methods of observation and analysis, including: reading widely in books written from all major world-view perspectives, and paying attention to what is going on in society and the world around us.

Two Basic Methods

The Christian mind begins with an attitude. But attitude is only the beginning. There must be some content, and some method toward getting that content. What are the first steps toward the specific formation of the Christian mind?

Two basic methods of analysis are involved, one using the tools of sociology, the other the tools of philosophy. The first involves reflecting on our actions as human beings. What we do and what our society does affects who we are and what we think. So we look at the cultural forces that mold us from the outside.

The second method of analysis involves reflecting on our basic intellectual commitments, the assumptions we make before we think. We look, in other words, at the inner workings of our minds. Both kinds of analysis are necessary to the development of a fully conscious Christian mind.

Using the tools of sociology—especially the sociology of knowledge—we can begin to see how such social forces as *individualism* or *pluralism* or *privatization* affect, not only the ways we act and think about ourselves and society, but even the ways we understand Scripture. We can discover that our very grasp of God's revelation is qualified by the social and cultural context in which we live. For example, so much are we influenced by the pervasiveness of individualism, especially in North America, that we see Paul's instructions to the church as a community as advice only to us as individuals. When Paul in Ephesians writes, "Put on the full armor of God so that you can take your stand against the devil's schemes" (Eph 6:11), we see ourselves as individuals putting on the armor. But the *you* here is plural in the Greek. It is first of all the church that is to put on the armor, not the individual. But John Wayne, the Lone Ranger, Lee Iacocca, Humphrey Bogart, Horatio Alger—all the heroes of our culture—lie in the background of our thought and affect our hermeneutic, our way of reading the Bible.

Using the tools of intellectual analysis, on the other hand, helps us see just what we are actually assuming before we do any thinking at all. Then we ask Scripture those tough questions whose answers should be at the root of our mindset. What is God really like? Who am I? Who are we all? How should we then live? When we use the tools of intellectual analysis well, we can deliberately shape our minds. Or better, through such reflection, God will shape our minds more and more into the image of his Son.

In this book we will use both sociological and intellectual tools, though the bulk of our attention will be placed on intellectual analysis. This is due in part to my own greater familiarity with intellectual matters and also to the fact that Christians, especially evangelical Christians, have paid much less attention to sociology and therefore much less is known about it. It is an area that needs the attention of God's people today. Perhaps some readers of this book will want to take up the challenge.[18]

A Brief Overview

We have begun our investigation of the Christian mind with the most important issue of all—our attitude toward God. Now we get on with charting its contours.

Chapters two through six are basic, designed to introduce the broad spectrum of a Christian mind. We first look at world views in general. What are the key ideas? How do we begin to think about our thinking? How do we become aware of what shapes our thoughts and actions?

Chapter seven turns to application—how should we then live? Its focus on technology gives an illustration of the Christian mind in operation. Chapter eight looks specifically at the academic enterprise, especially in the natural and human sciences. Chapter nine discusses the cultural enterprises of literature and the media. The final chapter looks back on the past and forward to the future as it surveys the scope of God's plan for the ages and our place in it. The appendix is a bonus for undergraduate students who want to see how they might apply the principles presented in this book toward wending their way through college. The bibliography at the end is simply the best general bibliography I know of toward the development of a discipled mind.

Developing a discipled mind is more than standing under a waterfall. But it is not less. So we take the plunge.

Every person carries in his head a mental model of the
world—a subjective representation of external reality.

Alvin Toffler[1]

Chapter 2
Mental Models of the World:
An Introduction to
World-View Analysis

*T*he Christian world view is only one among many in today's world. These mental models vary from culture to culture, society to society, and even from person to person. In the twentieth century, world views have in fact proliferated so much that we call our Western world pluralistic. Our culture has become almost as chaotic as the society depicted in the book of Judges. We, each of us, simply think and do whatever is right in our own eyes.

We all operate our lives out of our own mental model of the world, our own notion of what the world is really like. In other words, each of us has a world view.

What Is a World View?

What is a world view? Essentially this: *A world view is a set of presup-*

*positions (assumptions which may be true, partially true or entirely false)
which we hold (consciously or subconsciously, consistently or inconsistently)
about the basic makeup of our world.*[2]

Let us take up each part of this definition separately. A world view
is set of *presuppositions,* that is, a combination of fundamental commitments to the way we think things are. In a major sense these
presuppositions are pre-theoretical. We do not first get them by thinking about them. Rather, when we come to think about them, we find
them already there, already undergirding any thinking we do. Of
course, when we have once turned our attention to them, we can
began to think about them and consciously change them, if we wish.
But at first, we just identify that we have them and then discover what
they are.

Seven Basic World-View Questions

Next we note that these presuppositions are multiple; they form a *set
of assumptions* that are the foundation of all our thought. The set itself
can best be understood as our rock-bottom answers to seven basic
questions. In the chapters to follow we will look in detail at the various
answers that have been given to these questions. It suffices here, for
the purpose of definition, simply to identify the questions and give a
few very brief, sample answers.

1. *What is prime reality—the really real?* To this different people might
answer: God, or the gods, material cosmos or cosmic mind.

2. *What is the nature of external reality, that is, the world around us?*
Here different people's answers point to whether they see the world
as created or autonomous; as chaotic or orderly; as matter or spirit.
They also show whether they emphasize a subjective, personal relationship to the world or its objectivity apart from us.

3. *What is a human being?* To this different people might answer: a
highly complex machine, a sleeping god, a person made in the image
of God, a "naked ape."

4. *What happens to a person at death?* Here different people might reply: personal extinction, or transformation to a higher state, or departure to a shadowy existence on "the other side."

5. *Why is it possible to know anything at all?* Sample answers include the idea that human beings are made in the image of an all-knowing God or that consciousness and rationality developed under the contingencies of survival in a long process of evolution.

6. *How do we know what is right and wrong?* Again, perhaps we are made in the image of a God whose character is good; or right and wrong are determined by human choice alone; or the notions simply developed under an impetus toward cultural or physical survival.

7. *What is the meaning of human history?* To this different people might answer: to realize the purposes of God or the gods, to make a paradise on earth, to prepare a people for a life in community with a loving and holy God, and so forth.

More or Less Conscious, True, Consistent

Our own personal answers to these questions are our world view. But what a set of questions! They strike us with their depth, with the mystery that lies at the base of our answers to them, whatever those answers are. They are the toughest questions of life. So tough that, when we reflect on them, we may well give up trying to make sense of or be confident of our answers. That is, we are only more or less *conscious* of our world view.

Often in the process of growing up, we raise these questions with our parents or teachers or friends, and they look away embarrassed. They, no more than you, know how to answer them. Thus as children we often cease asking these questions of others and even of ourselves. Our budding critical mind shuts down. Cultural forces mold our actions and beliefs and, unless some crisis of life comes along—our best friend dies young, our own children go on drugs, we discover we have cancer—we never bother to ask the questions again.

By the time we are fully grown, even through college and into the workaday world, we may not be conscious of our answers to some of them at all. As Whitehead says, some "assumptions appear so obvious that people do not know what they are assuming because no other way of putting things has ever occurred to them."[3]

I suspect, for example, that most people today have at least once in their lifetime thought about whether God exists and, if not, then wondered how the universe came into being or continues to hang together. And many have wondered how they could find the answers to their questions about this. They have thought about gathering data and maybe making hypotheses about that data and then confirming their hypotheses with further thought and experiment. In other words, they may have a conscious grasp of some elements of the so-called scientific method and have thought about applying it to the question of God's existence. But I suspect that few have consciously asked how it is possible to know anything at all. We just know, don't we?

Moreover, each presupposition we make, each answer we give to these questions, is more or less *true*. Any given assumption we make about what is finally there—God or the universe or cosmic mind—is either true, partially true (needing considerable refinement) or entirely false. The notion, for example, that the universe is upheld by the Downers Grove frog god is certainly false. But does an infinite-personal God, say Yahweh or Allah, uphold the universe? That is not so easy to determine. Still, either he does or he doesn't, and the presupposition that he does is either true or false (or in need of further clarification so that we can be sure what is being asserted).

Finally, our presuppositions are either more or less *consistent* with each other. Some people, for example, do not believe in the supernatural or in the existence of a spiritual realm, yet they take comfort in the idea of reincarnation. But reincarnation implies precisely what the existence of either the supernatural or the spiritual realm affirms—a substratum of existence that is not material. They can't have it both ways. Some Christians have tried to blend reincarnation with their otherwise orthodox notions of God and human nature, and that, as we will see in chapter four, cannot be done consistently either.

The Christian World View

The Christian world view answers each of the seven questions with a fair degree of confidence. It claims the answers are true and consistent with each other. In light of all the confusion regarding these questions today, how is this possible? The world view itself explains why. God wants us to know these answers, and he has told us what the answers are.

The Christian world view's answer to the first question forms the basis for the answers to all the other questions, for what the Christian world view takes to be the really real is an infinite-personal God who intentionally made the universe and us in it. He wanted us around to freely know him, and so he built into us the capacity for knowledge.

But this is to get way ahead of ourselves. We need to back up before going on. The question of just what fundamental reality is is prior to how we know what fundamental reality is. So let us begin at the beginning.

I am the LORD, who has made all things, who alone
stretched out the heavens, who spread out the earth by
myself.

Isaiah 44:24

Chapter 3
The Final Reality:
The Beginning That
Has No Beginning

W hat is the beginning that has no beginning? Sounds like a riddle Rumpelstiltskin might ask—a conundrum, needing an answer like a circle or a sphere. Instead, it is the most important question our world view answers. The answer determines the shape of every answer to every other world-view question. Essentially what this question demands of us is a commitment to reality. After all that is finite and contingent has been transcended, what is the world like at its rootiest root? It is, in other words, a formulation of the first of two questions we will deal with in this chapter. Let's get them out on the table.

Question 1: What is prime reality—the really real?

Question 2: What is the nature of external reality, that is, the world around us? What kind of place do we live in, anyway?

An Elephant Story

There is a story that places these first two world-view questions in perspective.

One day a little boy came to his father and asked, "You know, Dad, our teacher just showed us that the world is really round and that it is just out there alone. Gee, Dad, what holds it up?"

His father thinking his son would be satisfied with a child's answer, said, "Well, son, a camel holds the world up." His son, always trusting his father, looked puzzled but walked away satisfied—for a while.

The next day after he thought this over, he came back to his Dad and asked the obvious question. "Dad, you know, you said yesterday the world rests on a camel. But what holds the camel up?"

His father, a bit perplexed, quickly thought, "You know, this kid's got a good question. I don't know the answer to it, but I'd better make up one—and fast." Like most fathers he knew instinctively that a quick answer turneth away further questions. So he said with confidence, "Son, a kangaroo holds the camel up."

So his son went away but returned a short time later and said, "Hey, Dad. I've still got a problem. What holds up the kangaroo?"

His father was now desperate, so he thought quickly and figured he would make one last try. So he searched his mind for the largest animal he could think of, and he put a capital[1] on it and said loudly (if you shout, people believe you): "An Elephant holds the world up."

"Come on, Dad," his son said, having now caught on that his father was not getting to the bottom of things, "what holds up the Elephant?"

So his father came back in an exasperated stroke of pure genius, "Son, it's Elephant all the way down."

A Sure-fire Test for Presuppositions

This story illustrates two very important ideas. First, it illustrates what a presupposition is. You know you have reached a presupposition when the only thing left to do is shout. A child asks, "Why, Mamma?" and eventually, after all the explanation she can give proves unsuccessful, she is forced to declare in a question-stopping voice: "Because! Just because!" One cannot endlessly pile animal after animal, reason after reason, on top of each other. One reaches a point at which there seems no way to go further. One cannot prove to oneself that that point is the final resting place. One just has to say, "That's it. I can go no further with my explanations. This will have to suffice until I think of something better."

Sagan or Kepler

Second, the Elephant story illustrates the kind of answer that applies to the first world-view question: *What is prime reality—the really real?* The question "What holds up the world?" is simply another way of asking, What is the basis for the way things are? What is the final reality that explains how things hold together?

Let us see what would have happened if the father in the Elephant story had taken an adult, say, scientific approach. Let's say that he had said to his son's first question, "The law of gravity holds the world in place."

"Gosh, Dad, what's that?"

"Well, it's rather complicated to explain, and it took us as a human race a long time to figure it out. But about three hundred years ago Isaac Newton finally did. The basic idea is this: $F = G(m_1 m_2)/R^2$. This obtains where F = the force of gravity; G = the gravitational constant; m_1 = the mass of body 1; m_2 = the mass of body 2; and R = the distance between m_1 and m_2.[2]

"Wow, Dad. That's impressive. But why is this so?"

His father could then say, "The law of gravity works because it is the expression of the uniformity of natural causes operating in the universe. You see, the universe is an orderly place. Things always work the same way under the same conditions. The law of gravity

simply expresses the principle of uniformity as regards the relationship between physical bodies in the universe."

Would not his son again ask, "Why, Dad?"

His father then would have to make a choice. He could end the
discussion in one of two ways. He could say, "Well, that's just the way
it is. That is the foundation principle of the universe: it's uniform all
the way down." That is, he could commit himself to the final reality
being the orderly structure of the material universe. That is in fact what
I think astrophysicist and scientific popularizer Carl Sagan would tell his
son, for Sagan opens his book and his TV series *Cosmos* with just such
a statement: "The Cosmos is all there is or ever was or ever will be."[3]

But there is a second possibility. He could go one step further,
saying, "Well, son that's the way God made the world. Isn't it wonderful! God is a rational God. The Bible even calls him Logos, logic itself.
So, of course, the world is orderly!" This is what scientist Johannes
Kepler would have told his son, for he once wrote in praise of God
the Creator, "O God, I am thinking thy thoughts after thee."[4]

Given the assumption that the earth and other astral bodies are
really "out there" as objective, material entities (a view which is possible to challenge, as we shall see in a moment), I don't see what other
alternatives would be available. Either the world is orderly on its own,
or it has been brought into being by a God who wanted it to be
orderly. Either answer on the surface of it is possible. Neither answer
can be proven. Both are presuppositions, pretheoretical commitments. As such they may both be tested—that is, one could see what
follows from each, and one of them might emerge as more likely to
be the case than the other, but it is in principle impossible to get
beneath either. To do so would be to be God, to be within oneself
cognizant of eternal matters.

The Great Divide: Theism, Naturalism or Pantheism

Though the variations within them are many indeed, in my estimation there are only three basic world views. When we answer the first world-view question, we have no choice but to commit ourselves to one of these views. In the Elephant story and its commentary we have seen the beginnings of two of them. The third we will introduce presently.

Theists like Kepler say that prime reality is an infinite-personal God. He alone exists forever. All that is not this God is the creation of this God.

Naturalists like Sagan say that prime reality is the cosmos itself.

Pantheists, at least one major segment of them, say prime reality is Brahman, the divine oneness that unifies everything. That is, God and the Cosmos are really one and the same.

The pantheist's answer may seem odd because the cosmos does not look like God to us. But that is so, the pantheist would say, because under ordinary circumstances (that is, when we trust our senses and our ability to reason), we are not actually in touch with reality. Our senses, including those that perceive the world as "out there" in space, separated from other astral bodies, are misleading us. The earth does not need to be held up by anything. The whole so-called physical universe is an illusion.

In terms of the Elephant story, a father who is this sort of pantheist might answer his son's question about what holds the world in space this way.

"Son, the earth, you know, is not really there at all. It is not so much hanging in space in and of itself as it simply appears to you and your teacher to be so."

"What do you mean, Dad? How is that an answer."

"There are no answers, Son. There should be no questions."

"Why, Dad?"

"That's a question, Son. You must learn not to ask questions."

"How, Dad?"

"There you go again! Come, let us sit together quietly. Let us breathe deeply, quietly. Let us look at this beautiful design, Son."

The end of such an approach is to put questions of all kinds on hold. To those of us raised in the Western world, the whole process seems wrong-headed. But it is taken very seriously by much of the world's population, and it has a sophisticated literature and a vast panorama of religious expressions. Hinduism and Buddhism in the many forms are fueled by this fundamental commitment to the notion that everything either is God, an emanation of God or total illusion. We look at other forms of pantheism below (pp. 44-46) in this chapter.

On the basis of their answer to the first world-view question, then, we have three possible basic world views. These can be diagrammed as in figure 1.

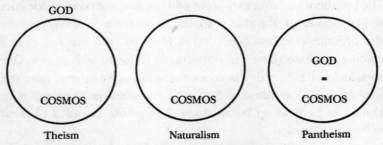

Figure 1. God and cosmos in theism, naturalism and pantheism.

God as the Really Real

Christianity is obviously a form of theism, though it is not the only example of theism. Two other major religions are theistic—Judaism and Islam. Within both these religions God is seen as prime reality. All else stems from him.

The differences between these three religions have to do with the character and nature of this God who is believed to exist. Christianity and Islam both accept much of the Hebrew Scripture's notion of God—his infinity, his absolute power, his sovereignty over his own creation, including humanity. But Islam holds that Muhammad was

God's special prophet who wrote the Koran by direct dictation from God and so the teachings of the Koran take precedence over the Hebrew Scriptures. Christianity, on the other hand, sees God as Trinity—Father, Son and Holy Spirit—and it emphasizes the incarnation of God the Son as Jesus Christ, who expressed God's love by dying for the sins of the people he created. Christians see both the teachings of Jesus and his apostles and the Hebrew Scriptures as authoritative.

In any case, it is not the differences between these forms of theism that will occupy us here. The important matter is the development of a Christian mind. So we will focus on the nature of God as Christians view him.

The God of the Old and New Testaments is *infinite* and *personal (Triune), transcendent* and *immanent, sovereign, omniscient* and *good.*[5] One classic Protestant definition of God is found in the Westminster Confession:

> There is but one living and true God, who is infinite in being and perfection, a most pure spirit, invisible, without body, parts or passions, immutable, immense, eternal, incomprehensible, almighty; most wise, most holy, most free, most absolute, working all things according to the counsel of his own immutable and most righteous will, for his own glory; most loving, gracious, merciful long-suffering, abundant in goodness and truth, forgiving iniquity, transgression and sin; the rewarder of them that diligently seek him; and withal most just and terrible in his judgments; hating all sin, and who will by no means clear the guilty.[6]

We saw in the Elephant story a little of what it means for God to be *infinite.* He is the final reality, the only self-existent being. As Jehovah God spoke to Moses out of the burning bush, "I AM WHO I AM" (Ex 3:14). He *is* in a way that none else is. As Moses proclaimed, "Hear, O Israel: The LORD our God, the LORD is one" (Deut 6:4). So God is the one prime existent, the one prime reality and, as we shall develop later, the one source of all other reality.

God is *personal*. This means God is not mere force or energy or existent "substance." Rather, he has the two basic characteristics of personality: (1) self-reflection and (2) self-determination. He knows himself to be, and he is an agent of action. He is not compelled by anything external to himself but can freely determine what he wishes and act as he chooses.

The personhood of God is expressed in the *Trinity*, three "persons," Father, Son and Holy Spirit, yet one as God. As theologian Geoffrey W. Bromiley says, "Within the one essence of the Godhead we have to distinguish three 'persons' who are neither three gods on the one side, not three parts or modes of God on the other, but coequally and coeternally God."[7] The Trinity confirms the communal, "personal" nature of ultimate being. God is not only there—an actually existent being—he is personal, and we can relate to him in a personal way.

God is also *transcendent*. This means God is beyond us and our world. He is *otherly*. He is not a part of the cosmos, nor are we a part of him. The ancient Hebrew psalmist wrote,

I lift up my eyes to the hills—
where does my help come from?
And he quickly answers,
My help comes from the LORD,
the Maker of heaven and earth. (Ps 121:1-2)

There has been a long and deep strain of pantheism in human history even in the West. Think, for example, of William Wordsworth, in England, and Ralph Waldo Emerson, Henry David Thoreau and Walt Whitman, in America, and more recently the literature of the beat generation—Jack Kerouac and Gary Snyder. Nature for these authors takes on a cast of the divine. It would be from the spirit of the hills themselves that these authors would seek help. But the God of the Bible is transcendent. God is not the hills; he is beyond them. He is otherly, as some theologians put it.

Yet it is still true that God is constantly present to all his creation. God is indeed not only transcendent but *immanent* as well. Look at a hill: God is present. Look at a person: God is present. Is this, then, a contradiction? Is theism nonsense at this point? I think not.

Is God *here* in the same way a hill is here? No, not quite. God is immanent, here, everywhere, in a sense completely in line with his transcendence. For God is not *matter,* but Spirit. A text from the book of Hebrews states it this way: Jesus Christ is said to be "upholding the universe by his word of power" (Heb 1:3 RSV). That is, God is beyond all, yet in all and sustaining all.

God is also *sovereign.* This is really a further ramification of God's infiniteness, but it expresses more fully his concern to rule, to pay attention, as it were, to all the actions of his universe. It expresses the fact that nothing is beyond God's ultimate interest, control and authority.

God is likewise both *omniscient* and *good.* These are characteristics we will look at further in chapters five and six respectively.

And that brings us to the second world-view question: What is the nature of external reality?

We will begin to answer the second question by making a comparison again between the three world views. This time we will look at other forms of pantheism than the one we have just seen above. But let's take the simplest one first.

The Cosmos on Its Own
Naturalists hold that the cosmos itself is eternal. That means that for the naturalist the answer to the first two world-view questions is the same.

True, the cosmos has not always been in its present form, and its form is constantly changing, at least from our point of view. But the natural order of things (the matter/energy complex)—that is all there is. The cosmos is closed off from any influence from the outside; in fact, there is no outside. There is a uniformity of natural causes in a totally closed system. In such a system, of course, there can be no miracle. Anything that looks a miracle is merely the result of natural causes we have not yet understood.

For naturalists, therefore, all explanations of how things are have to be made in terms of the natural order. If something moves, it moves because of its place in the natural scheme. If someone has an idea, it is because of the inherent character of the natural world. If someone believes there is something outside the cosmos, then that belief must be explained in terms of the natural world. God is never seen to be the cause of the idea of God. Rather the idea of a God outside the cosmos is caused by something within the cosmos itself. Naturalists, therefore, have sociologies of religion and psychologies of religion (the subject of both of which include belief in God) but never theologies (for theologies have God for their subject and God doesn't exist).

This fact, by the way, explains the frequent frustration of many Christians who study social science in the university. It seems to them as if their religious views are never taken as serious contenders for truth. This is so not because their teachers have it in for them, so to speak, but because these teachers have ruled out from the start any possibility that any religious idea could be true. We have here what Stephen Eyre calls the socialization of unbelief.[8] When Christian students understand this, they can get on with the task of learning from their courses despite the prejudice against their views.[9] The fact is that their teachers are often ignorant of the contributions of thoughtful Christians to the social sciences. And many as well are ignorant of what genuine biblical Christianity is.

The Cosmos as Divine

Pantheists, at least a very large portion of them, hold that the external world is really illusory. The cosmos is a projection of God, somehow equal to God, in as much as it exists, but totally illusory as objective in and of itself.

The key phrase in this form of pantheism is *Atman is Brahman,* a phrase coming from The Upanishads, one of the Hindu scriptures. That is, Atman (the soul of any one person or thing) is Brahman (God, the Soul of everything). In the nondualist form of pantheism, all things in as much as they are differentiated from each other are illusory. Brahman (prime reality) is one and one alone. Sometimes the external world is said to be the dream of God or an emanation from God or an extension of God. It is not, however, God's creation; it is, in as much as it is at all, a part of God. Of course, because Brahman is the unitary one, it is also appropriate to say the external universe is not Brahman but rather illusion.

Do not be discouraged if you have found the above two paragraphs difficult to comprehend. The nondualist form of pantheism (one of its major expressions) is not capable of being understood by normal intellectual processes. One has to pass, so these pantheists say, beyond the mind and grasp the matter intuitively. Meditation replaces thought as a way of getting to the bottom of things.

There are other ways of formulating the pantheist answer to what is the really real. The Buddhists, for instance, take a radically different notion of what this oneness at the root of reality is. For them it is the Void—the nothingness from which all illusory forms come. Each person, each self, is not Atman (soul); each self is really not-self, a kind of undifferentiated nothingness. From such a conception stems a very different form of religion (if Buddhism can be called a religion, since it really does not believe in any kind of God at all).

One can also hold dualist forms of pantheism. Here God and the cosmos are held to be the same, but genuine existence is granted to a multiplicity of forms. Animism—the idea that nature has a divine substratum, that spirits live in trees, rivers and all natural forms—is a subspecies of pantheism that does not so much emphasize the unity of reality as its diversity. Some "nature lovers" too modern to believe that spirits live in trees nonetheless see nature itself as divine. Animals (baby seals and whales, for example) have as much right to life as we.

One of the most interesting forms pantheism has taken recently is the Gaia hypothesis.[10] Gaia is the name of the ancient Greek Earth goddess. Some scientists are proposing that the Earth itself is somehow alive, a single giant organism, or maybe even a single cell, of which the various life forms are a part. Biologist and medical doctor Lewis Thomas muses:

> I have been trying to think of the earth as a kind of organism, but it is no go. I cannot think of it this way. It is too big, too complex, with too many working parts lacking visible connections. The other night, driving through a hilly, wooded part of southern New England, I wondered about this. If not like an organism, what is it like, what is it *most* like? Then, satisfactorily for that moment, it came to me: it is *most* like a single cell.[11]

This single cell, in Thomas's musings, begins to take on the characteristics of at least a lesser God. He talks of DNA being an *invention* of nature *designed* for a specific task, of human beings as made for a purpose—to have language that is ambiguous so that we can invent and imagine and create.[12] And he even speculates that at death the human consciousness is "somehow separated off at the filaments of its attachment, and then drawn like an easy breath back into the membrane of its origin, a fresh memory for the biospherical nervous system." Then tellingly he adds, "but I have no data on the matter."[13]

Lewis comes close to talking about a cosmic mind, a thoughtfulness in the universe, a central controlling intelligence which, while it may not be fully personal or endowed with loving intentions, nonetheless "holds up the world" and suggests a modicum of purpose to reality. What ever form it takes, pantheism, without recognizing the existence of a transcendent God, endows the cosmos with the aura of divinity.

The Cosmos as Created

Theists hold that the external world is a deliberate, designed orderly creation of God over which his sovereignty continues to extend.

The opening text of the Bible says it most succinctly: "In the beginning God created the heavens and the earth" (Gen 1:1). The verses that follow give an account of the orderly progression of God's creative activity. And Isaiah echoes this in many ways, not the least in this passage:

I am the LORD,
who has made all things,
who alone stretched out the heavens,
who spread out the earth by myself. (Is 44:24)

It is a view made for poetry, and Scripture abounds in rhapsodic song:

O LORD my God, you are very great;
you are clothed with splendor and majesty.
He wraps himself in light as with a garment;
he stretches out the heavens like a tent
and lays the beams of his upper chambers on their waters.
He makes the clouds his chariot
and rides on the wings of the wind.
He makes winds his messengers,
flames of fire his servants.
He set the earth on its foundations;
it can never be moved. (Ps 104:1-5)

Notice how the last line, without stopping to contemplate the role of gravity (Newtonian or Einsteinian), simply answers our young boy's question. Who holds the world in place? God himself. He made it. He takes care of it.

The heavens declare the glory of God;
the skies proclaim the work of his hands. (Ps 19:1)

The notion of God as Creator, however, is not just a matter for poetic ecstasy. There is no notion more important to the Christian mind than the notion of God as Creator. Let us look at *two* reasons this is so.

First, the notion of God as Creator puts us in our place. God is God; we are not. Everything we are and have belongs to him. We own nothing that is not his—our bodies, our souls, our minds, our emotions, our thoughts. And that is true for everyone whether they know it or not.

We cannot escape his presence. If he should forget about us, we would cease to exist. This is both terrifying and comforting.

> Where can I go from your Spirit?
> Where can I flee from your presence? . . .
> If I say, "Surely the darkness will hide me
> and the light become night around me,"
> even the darkness will not be dark to you;
> the night will shine like the day,
> for darkness is as light to you. (Ps 139: 7, 11-12)

It is terrifying to think that there is nothing God does not know about us, for what we ourselves know about us is bad enough. Our sins are an open book for him to read and weep—and worse! Even our goodness is like filthy rags (Is 64:6). But his constant presence is also comforting. It is comforting to know that God in his mercy is so gracious to us that he puts our sins as far away from him as is the east from the west (Ps 103:12). The contemplation of his presence indeed brings us to the *fear of the Lord,* which is, as we saw, the beginning of knowledge.

Second, the notion of God as Creator affects the way we think about everything. If God is really the creator of everything other than himself, then our understanding of anything will be incomplete and maybe quite inaccurate unless we take into account his presence as Creator. Upon hearing him present one of his scientific theories, Napoleon once asked P. S. Laplace (1749-1827) where God was in all of his explanation. Laplace replied, "I have no need of God in my hypotheses." Laplace may have been right, so long as he limited himself to purely physical bodies and the structure of their relationship to each other. But the bodies wouldn't be there without God, nor would Laplace or Napoleon. There would be no thought to think, no hypothesis making, no question asking, nothing at all.

Much modern thought, however, assumes that Laplace is right in the ultimate and absolute sense. Naturalism exalts Laplace's answer to a metaphysical principle. As much as we as Christians can respect much of the work of modern science, we cannot marginalize God or push him to the edge of our minds when we do science. He must be the hidden premise of all our work as scholars. He is the reason the world is orderly and therefore capable of being understood. (We will return to this notion in chapters five, eight and nine.)

Third, the notion of God as creator affects the way we understand what the universe is like. God is totally free to make any kind of universe he chooses to make. It is an orderly universe because he is a rational God. But it does not have to have any specific pattern. That is, the order in his creation may not be presumed.

In medieval thought the circle was considered the perfect geometrical form. God made the heavens; the heavens, unlike the earth, are not fallen but perfect; perfect motion is motion in a circle; therefore, the orbits of the planets must be circular. Johannes Kepler went even further. He argued that since God is orderly (actually, a mathematician), then the planets must not only inscribe circular orbits, but also orbits which have a tidy but subtle relationship to the perfect solids. His particular views are too complex to be described here. The point is that the facts Kepler had available came close to justifying his theory but not close enough to constitute a proof. Finally Kepler gave up his theory in the face of the facts. When Kepler considered sufficient data, he discovered that the planets moved in elliptic, not circular orbits.

So the idea of the universe as created means that (1) it actually exists

apart from any human observer and is not just an illusion; (2) it is
orderly; and (3) it is contingent (its specific form is not *necessary*). As
Charles Hummel says, "The dependence of such beliefs, both histor-
ically and philosophically, on the biblical doctrine of creation leads
directly to the role of Christianity in the scientific revolution."[14]

So then, what is the nature of external reality? External reality is
creation. And since this creation is the result of the design of a rational God, it is orderly—*a uniformity of natural causes in an open system.*
That is, in addition to being orderly, it is always open to its creator
for reordering and to any personal beings to whom its creator gives
power. Miracles are possible in a theistic universe because God can
always do whatever he chooses. These miracles are not, of course,
illogical or irrational, because the creator is not illogical or irrational.
They may occur seldom or often. They may be understood by people
or not understood, but when the latter is the case it will not be due
to the illogic of the miracle but to the inability of the human mind
always to understand its maker.[15]

The World-View Matrix

Our discussion of these first two questions illustrates an important
feature of world views. The answer they give to one question affects
the answers they give to all the other questions one can ask. Naturalism's answer to question 2 is in fact the same as it is to question 1.
And given theism's answer to question 1, the cosmos has to have been
created. For if both God and the cosmos exist now, and if the cosmos
did not always exist, then the only way it could have come into being
is if God created it.

As Christians we want to learn, as Kepler said, to think God's
thoughts after him. God is rational; therefore, we should be rational.
Our world view, then, should be both consistent and coherent. That
is, not only should it not contain any contradictions, but it should be
composed of presuppositions which fit well together, presuppositions

which, because they are as correct as we can get them, give us a coherent picture of the way things really are.

This is a tall order—too tall to be accomplished in this lifetime. Yet we can try. At least we can make a stab at thinking our way around the next two world-view questions.

A thing there is whose voice is one,
Whose feet are two and four and three.
So mutable a thing is none
That moves in earth or sky or sea.
When on most feet this thing doth go
Its strength is weakest and its pace most slow.

The Riddle of the Sphinx[1]

Chapter 4
The Riddle of the World:
The Nature
of Human Nature

Oedipus, the ancient mythological king of Thebes, achieved his fame by solving the riddle of the Sphinx (see p. 51). That freed his city from bondage to this powerful goddess from the underworld. The answer was Man: for man goes on all fours when a baby, on two feet as an adult, and on three feet (with a cane) when old.

But what is the solution to the riddle of Man—the riddle of human nature? If we are the riddle of the world, who are we?

The answer we give to this question is second only in importance to our conception of fundamental reality. It sets the tone for our understanding of ourselves and all the human relations that go to make up our lives.

In this chapter, then, we will take up the Christian answer to the riddle of human nature and place it in the context of alternative answers. In short, we will deal with the answers to the next two of the seven world-view questions.

Question 3: What is a human being?

Question 4: What happens to a person at death?

In His Image

Christians do not have to read far into the Bible to find the most important clue to human nature. The first chapter of Genesis lays down the base line.

> Then God said, "Let us make man in our image, in our likeness, and let them rule over the fish of the sea and the birds of the air, over the livestock, over all the earth, and over all the creatures that move along the ground."
>
> So God created man in his own image,
> in the image of God he created him;
> male and female he created them. (Gen 1:26-27)

Two terms of this text stand out. Human beings are (1) *created* in the (2) *image of God.*

That we are *created* means that we are not on our own in any sense at all. We are obligated to God in every possible way. Were it not for his decision to have made us, we would not be. Everything we are is his. Our freedom to think and choose and make significant decisions—even our ability to say no to God—derives from him. From the fact of our creation derives the necessity for humility.

Also because of their belief in creation Christians reject both the naturalist and the pantheist notions of human beings. For the *naturalist* we are simply the product of the cosmos doing its thing without intention or design. *Homo sapiens* came on the scene as the result of a long process of evolution. There was no particular reason for the coming of human beings or for their development of culture.

Loren Eisley, as enraptured as he is by the cosmos and human beings in it, recognizes the plight this view puts us in:

[What we have in nature is] absolute random novelty.... Man has ... been moving in a world of contingent forms. ... The brain of man, that strange gray iceberg of conscious and unconscious life, was similarly unpredictable until its appearance.[2]

And Eisley concludes:

Man [is] ... a homeless orphan lost in the vast abysses of space and time.... Our universe, ... however strung with connecting threads, is endowed with an open-ended and perverse quality we shall never completely master. Nature contains that which does not concern us, and has no intention of taking us into its confidence.[3]

This is far too low a view of human nature. We are more than "natural"; we are "supernatural," not that we are gods but that we are the intended creation of God. We are to be explained not solely by "natural" processes but by divine intention. God wanted us to be. We must, of course, be careful not to think that anything in the natural order of the universe exists apart from God. The whole of what we commonly call nature is created and exists, as we saw in chapter two, solely because he wants it to.

For a *pantheist,* human beings are in themselves God, or a spark of God. This is in one sense too high a view of human nature. It leads to the ultimate form of pride, hubris, making us think of ourselves as more than we ought. Worse, it dethrones God and deprives him of his glory. As we shall see below, it is the primal sin to hold this view.

But there is more to the Christian notion of human nature than that we were created. That we are made *in the image of God* means that we are significantly different from the rest of creation. All of creation bears some semblance of God. But we are more like God than anything else. From this notion derives our human dignity.

The psalmist reflects on this amazing fact: somehow, as magnificent as the night skies are, as much as they humble us with their awesome

majesty, we lowly human beings have a special place in the vast
scheme of things.

> You made him a little lower than God[4]
>   and crowned him with glory and honor.
> You made him ruler over the works of your hands;
>   you put everything under his feet:
> all flocks and herds,
>   and the beasts of the field,
> the birds of the air,
>   and the fish of the sea;
>   all that swim the paths of the seas. (Ps 8:5-8)

Male and Female

One of the most important characteristics of human beings is the fact
that we are communal. In the context of telling us that God created
us in his own image, Genesis 1:27 says, God created us "male and
female." Our very diversity as men and women is a reflection of God's
nature. This tells us both something about us and about God.

About us we learn that there is a commonality to human beings that
transcends our sexuality. Men and women are both in God's image.
It is not man or woman first in hierarchy; it is both one and the other.
Moreover, the image of God is not expressed in the individual alone
but in the corporate male/female complex, in other words, in community.

About God we learn that he is not an integer, a oneness without
differentiation (as in Brahman). God himself is characterized by multiplicity. And that makes sense because personal beings require multiplicity in their nature. To be self-conscious, know themselves as
selves, there must be a part of them that knows another part, so to
speak. To have self-determination, God needs to be free to choose
between alternatives. This is indeed the kind of God we see him to
be throughout the pages of the Bible. In the New Testament we meet

him in full Trinitarian form—a unity of three persons—Father, Son and Holy Spirit. Human community on earth is reflected in community in heaven.

The creation story of Genesis 1 focuses on the cosmos, putting human beings as the highest creation on the last day of creation. The creation story of Genesis 2 focuses on the making of Adam and Eve.

And the LORD God formed man from the dust of the ground and breathed into his nostrils the breath of life, and man became a living being. (Gen 2:7)

God then planted a garden, put man in it, charged him with caring for it, and gave him free reign to eat of it as he wanted except for the tree of the knowledge of good and evil. Then God said, "It is not good for man to be alone. I will make a helper suitable for him." But first he made the animals and asked the man to name them.

But for Adam no suitable helper was found. So the LORD God caused the man to fall into a deep sleep; and while he was sleeping, he took one of the man's ribs and closed up the place with flesh. Then the LORD God made a woman from the rib he had taken out of the man, and he brought her to the man.

The man said,

"This is now bone of my bones
    and flesh of my flesh;
she shall be called 'woman,'
    for she was taken out of man."

For this reason a man will leave his father and mother and be united to his wife, and they will become one flesh.

(Gen 2:20-24)

As in Genesis 1, we find an emphasis on the mutual humanity of men and women. It is not good to be alone. People are made for others like themselves, but different. Though Adam and Eve were part and parcel of each other, Eve was not genetically cloned from Adam.

There is a difference and on that difference families are made. Men leave their homes and set up new families with their wives. The basic unit of society, then, is not the nation or tribe, on the one hand, or the individual, on the other; it is the family, a family composed at heart of two people who are themselves individuals (each different from the other) but made for each other.

This basic understanding of human nature should be at the heart of any Christian understanding of individuals in society.

Individualism: My Unconquerable Soul

The notion of *community* is very difficult for many of us to grasp emotionally. *Individualism* is for Americans a "habit of the heart."[5] To see how this is so it is helpful to use the insights of sociology.

Basically individualism proclaims: "I am self-sufficient. I need not, I ought not, depend on anyone but myself. I am in charge of my life. Who am I? Whatever I make myself to be. I do not get my identity from being a part of a group, whether humanity, nation, tribe or family." This is the fundamental conception of individualism, what, in fact, sociologist Robert Bellah and his colleagues at the University of California call *ontological individualism* (a concept held by philosopher John Locke).

In *ontological individualism* "the individual is prior to society, which comes into existence only through the voluntary contract of individuals trying to maximize their own self-interest."[6] The idea is this: before society comes the individual. Society is just an aggregate of individuals; it has no status other than that which individuals give it voluntarily. Human beings, in this view, are not essentially communal. They are essentially individual.

It may help to contrast this generally Western notion of human nature with the generally Eastern notion. Crudely put, in the West and especially since the Reformation and among Protestants, each human being is seen to be ontologically distinct. One's ego is bounded by one's skin. Society, then, is an aggregate of individuals who make an implicit social contract to be together and form voluntary associations. We might see this as in figure 2.

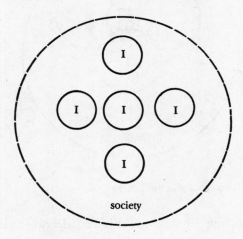

Figure 2. Individuals and society in the Western view.

In the East, each person is, of course, in many senses an individual, but that individuality is bound up with immediate and extended family. Each person is who he or she is only by virtue of relationships with others. Society is ontologically prior to the individual. The situation can be seen as in figure 3.

The best illustration of this is the difference in marriage customs between America and China (even between Americans with a European heritage and Americans with a Chinese heritage). What does it take to get married with society's blessing? My wife and I were anxious to get our parents' general blessing. I even asked her father's permission. But neither of us dreamed we would not get that permission, nor would it have stopped us from getting married if they had disap-

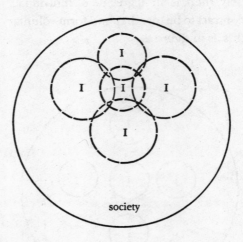

Figure 3: Individuals and society in the Eastern view.

proved. None of our friends would have paid any attention to the
nonapproval of our parents. Lincoln, Nebraska, society wouldn't have
blinked an eye.

But if our parents had come from China, they might have arranged
for us to marry someone else. If not, they might have disapproved of
our marriage. Their friends and maybe even some of ours would
have been scandalized by the thought of going ahead with our private
plans. Built into the Chinese conception of what it means to be human is a great respect for family, for society. Each person is not just
an individual but a member of a family that extends outward
into surrounding society. Society is ontologically prior to the individual.

Not so in the tradition of the West. Although Bellah does not give
this as an illustration, I think that "Invictus" by William Ernest Henley
(1849-1903) illustrates the extent to which Western ontological individualism is prepared to go.

Out of the night that covers me.
  Black as the Pit from pole to pole.
I thank whatever gods may be
  For my unconquerable soul.

In the fell clutch of circumstance
  I have not winced nor cried aloud.
Under the bludgeonings of chance
  My head is bloody but unbowed.

Beyond this place of wrath and tears
  Looms but the Horror of the shade,
And yet the menace of the years
  Finds, shall find, me unafraid.

It matters not how strait the gate,
  How charged with punishments the scroll,
I am the master of my fate;
  I am the captain of my soul.

Henley's form of individualism is, of course, extreme. It assumes a naturalistic universe or at least one in which he, Henley, has control over his own life and destiny. So, even though the notion of ontological individualism may unwittingly undergird our own understanding of the relationship between ourselves and society, we are unlikely to express it so baldly. But it helps to see our views at their extremities, if only to see where they would take us if we let them and to see that there may well be more of Henley in us than we would like to think.

Two Subspecies of Individualism: Utilitarian and Expressive
There are two subspecies of individualism we should also look at— utilitarian and expressive individualism.

In *utilitarian individualism* each individual is seen to have the opportunity to get ahead on his or her own initiative. It produces "a society where each vigorously pursue[s] his own interest."[7] This view "has an affinity to a basically economic understanding of human existence." Success is measured by material acquisitions, social power and prestige.

Benjamin Franklin's *Autobiography,* which is often taught in high school and offered as a model, is shot through with this notion. But in the 1980s it has come to be called the yuppie view—the values of the young, upwardly mobile, urban professional. Sadly, while this set of values could not be further from those espoused by Jesus, they tend nonetheless to be the values of Christians in developed countries all over the world. Its essential affinity, however, is with naturalism, not Christian theism. "Matter is all that matters" is a natural expression of the metaphysical notion that "Matter is all there is."

In *expressive individualism* each individual is free to "cultivate and express the self and explore its vast social and cosmic identities."[8] One is considered "free to express oneself, against all constraints and conventions."[9] Walt Whitman is one the early prime exponents of this view. Note, for example, these lines from his "Passage to India":[10]

Passage indeed O soul to primal thought,
Nor lands and seas alone, thy own clear freshness,
The young maturity of brood and bloom,
To realms of budding bibles.

O soul, repressless, I with thee and thou with me,
Thy circumnavigation of the world begin,
Of man, the voyage of his mind's return,
To reason's early paradise,
Back, back to wisdom's birth, to innocent intuitions,
Again with fair creation.

Or again these opening lines from "Song of the Open Road":

Afoot and light-hearted I take to the open road,

Healthy, free, the world before me,

The long brown path before me, leading wherever I choose.

Whitman in these passages clearly presupposes a pantheistic world view. Whitman's repressless soul is divine, limitless, unprescribed. He can go anywhere, do anything, be anything.[11]

Bellah shows how individualism in its many and various forms permeates American social reality. Christians are not immune from simply absorbing it into their understanding of faith. Whether Catholic, evangelical, mainline, liberal or conservative, Christians see themselves as individuals first and communities second. "Today religion in America is as private and diverse as New England colonial religion was public and unified," Bellah writes.[12] Some believers, like Sheila Larson, even admit to fashioning their own faith from scratch.

I believe in God. I'm not a religious fanatic. I can't remember the last time I went to church. My faith has carried me a long way. It's Sheilaism. Just my own little voice.[13]

Even when we realize that God is God and we are not, we see ourselves before God as an individual before an individual. Our faith tends to be a Lone Ranger Christianity. We sing, "I come to the garden alone," or "Just a closer walk with thee," or

On the Jericho road

there's room for just two.

No more or no less,

just Jesus and you.

The idea is even sometimes reflected in the names we call ourselves. There is, for example, a group of college students who call their organization MAG, short for Me and God. The idea of God relating to one's family or church is present but secondary. When we notice this and look again at the Bible, we see a very different picture.

Biblical Individualism and Community

The Christian world view avoids the fatal traps of both individualism and collectivism. It declares from the outset that each of us is unique and in the image of God, but that the God in whose image we are made is communal. That is, at our core, we are social beings. We were made for God; we were made for each other.

Most Western Christians are so aware of the value the Bible puts on the individual that I need only give a few illustrations. In the Old Testament, for instance, great emphasis is put on the leaders of the people. Moses, Aaron, Joshua, Gideon, Samson, David, Jonathan, Jeremiah—there is no mistaking their individual character. God speaks to them and through them, but their personalities shine through even the words they use to convey the Word of the Lord. Each person is seen to be responsible to God. No one can use the excuse that someone else is responsible for their sin. Our Grand Father himself, Adam, tried that; his argument with God was to no avail. Both he and our Grand Mother, Eve, suffered the consequences of the primal sin.

In the New Testament too, many of the characters of the Gospels are well-defined individuals—John the Baptist, the apostles Peter, John and Paul, for example. And most importantly, Jesus himself is an individual man who treated each person as an individual. Each answer was keyed to the person who asked it. There was no universal blanket message, given always in the same words to everyone. The good news of the kingdom of God as Jesus preached and enacted it shows the balance. It was for individuals in community. Likewise, the apostle Paul's letters, while written mostly for churches, groups of people, contain frequent messages for individuals he has met on his journeys. There is no gainsaying the value the Scriptures put on each specific person in the whole world.

It is the community side of the equation that we in our Western mode have missed. In fact, we tend to confuse *personal* with *individual,* so that we think that to be personal we have to emphasize our separateness, our distinctness as individuals. Actually we are never more personal than when we are in community.

We have already seen how the corporate aspect of human nature has been expressed in Genesis. Notice now how it is expressed elsewhere in the Old Testament. First, we see community in God's offer of salvation. "I will walk among you and be your God, and you will be my people" (Lev 26:12).

Second, we see it in prayers for deliverance. The psalms, a repository of many of the more individual and intimate prayers and pleas, contain countless commentaries on the corporate aspect of Jewish faith. In one of the psalms most relevant to our discussion here, the psalmist, even as he asks for individual help, puts his request in the context of community.

Remember me, O LORD, when you show favor to your people,
    come to my aid when you save them,
that I may enjoy the prosperity of your chosen ones,
    that I may share in the joy of your nation
    and join your inheritance in giving praise. (Ps 106:4-5)

Finally, we even see community in prayers of confession. Daniel and Nehemiah both confess the sins of the nation. Daniel prays,

We have been wicked and have rebelled; we have turned away from your commands and laws. We have not listened to your servants the prophets, who spoke in your name to our kings, our princes and our fathers, and to all the people of the land. (Dan 9:5)

The "our kings, our princes and our fathers" includes the sins of those who died before Daniel was even born. And Nehemiah likewise makes his confession all inclusive of himself, his contemporaries and his forebears.

I confess the sins we Israelites, including myself and my father's house, have committed against you. (Neh 1:6)

In short, "Old Testament faith," as Eichrodt says, "knows nothing in any situation or at any time of a religious individualism which gives

a man a private relationship with God unconnected with the community either in its roots, its realisation, or its goal."[14]

In the New Testament we see the same kinds of emphases. To
Joseph the angel announces that Jesus will "save his *people* from their
sins" (Mt 1:21). Jesus called *twelve disciples.* They were to pray "*Our*
father . . ." (Mt 6:9). After the resurrection the *church* comes into being,
a social unit which the apostle Peter described like this:

> You are a chosen *people,* a royal *priesthood,* a holy *nation,* a *people*
> belonging to God, that you may declare the praises of him who
> called you out of darkness into his wonderful light. (1 Pet 2:9—
> emphasis mine)

All these terms—*people, priesthood, nation*—are corporate. It is within
this context that the apostle Paul writes that "God works *among you* to
accomplish his purpose" (Phil 2:13).[15] We are indeed corporately one.

Perhaps the most striking biblical treatment of community, however, is in 1 Corinthians 12. That letter opens with a direct challenge
to the chaotic condition of the church in Corinth. Paul appeals to the
people not to divide into those who "follow Paul" or "follow Apollos"
or "follow Cephas" (1 Cor 1:10-13). Then he instructs them in some
basic but very practical theology, rechallenging them (in chapter 3 to
cease their divisiveness) and helping them deal with the problems of
living and worshiping God together.

In chapter 12, Paul paints a vivid picture of the church as a single
body with many members. It comes in the context of a discussion of
spiritual gifts.

> Now the body is not made up of one part but of many. If the foot
> should say, "Because I am not a hand, I do not belong to the body,"
> it would not for that reason cease to be part of the body. And if
> the ear should say, "Because I am not an eye, I do not belong to
> the body," it would not for that reason cease to be a part of the
> body. If the whole body were an eye, where would the sense of
> hearing be? If the whole body were an ear, where would the sense

of smell be? But in fact God has arranged the parts in the body, everyone of them, just as he wanted them to be. If they were all one part, where would the body be? (1 Cor 12:14-19)
This passage balances unity and diversity within the "body of Christ." In short, there is one body, many members. And Paul points out in the section that follows that all members are equally honorable and needed and that, though all have dignity, none should be proud. The Spirit which binds the body into one gives at least one spiritual gift to each person, but for the "common good," not private use or personal glory.

I have concentrated on the issue of individualism and community at considerable length because it is so vital for us to grasp. All human beings, not just Christians, are individuals with a social nature. That is to be the root presupposition of any Christian's world view regarding human nature. It will affect the way we think and act throughout our lives.

The Cultural Mandate
So we are made in God's image. So that image involves sexual differentiation, family, corporateness and individuality. That doesn't tell us what our purpose is. What are we for anyway?

Genesis 1 says that in the beginning of the human race, God "blessed" his human creation and told them: "Be fruitful and increase in number; fill the earth and subdue it. Rule over the fish of the sea and the birds of the air and over every living creature that moves on the ground" (v. 28) Then he gave Adam and Eve and the other animals the plants for food.

Genesis 2 is similar: "The LORD God took the man and put him in the Garden of Eden to work it and take care of it" (v. 15). Tending the garden has come in theology to be called the *cultural mandate*— a mandate that initiates the human trek from garden to city, for once one begins to fill the earth with people and to cultivate gardens, culture begins to form, civilization arises. The role of technology as an aspect of the cultural mandate will be discussed in chapter seven (pages 133-36).

The sad fact is, however, that Adam and Eve did not get very far toward fulfilling the mandate before they violated the one command they were to obey: "You are free to eat from any tree in the garden; but you must not eat from the tree of the knowledge of good and evil, for when you eat of it you will surely die" (Gen 2:16-17). When Adam and Eve ate the fruit, the cultural mandate got turned on its head. They became subject to nature, living after their own fallen passions. In stead of caring for the garden, they were forced out of it and their progeny (of which we are a part) ended up exploiting it.

God's purpose for humanity, therefore, did not get accomplished in the first instance. And it is too late now to repair matters on our own. Though the cultural mandate is still in effect, the context in which we are to fulfill it has changed. The ground is cursed and only "through painful toil will you eat of it" (Gen 3: 17). Our purpose, then, expands beyond the cultural mandate.

If we look again at the creation account, we find another clue to our purpose. Genesis 1 tells us that we are made in the image of God. If that is the case, we ought really to be who we were created to be. In short, our purpose is to be like God, to reflect his nature and character. God is the glorious infinite-personal Creator of us and all the cosmos; therefore we should reveal God's glory.

The Westminster Shorter Catechism asks, "What is the chief end of man?" and answers, "The chief end of man is to glorify God and enjoy him for ever." There is, of course, nothing we can do to make God glorious. "God is glorious. He simply needs to show Himself as He is. . . . That is what he does in man."[16]

What aspects of God, then, can we reflect? Some aspects we automatically reflect: he exists eternally; we exist temporally. He is all powerful; we have some power. He has total dominion; we are to exercise stewardship, a derived dominion, over the natural world. He knows all things; we know some things. He makes decisions in total freedom according to his perfect judgment; we make decisions according to our judgment.

And it is here, I believe, that our task begins. We are given the ability by God to make responsible decisions and to act on them. What kind of decisions should we make? The sorts of decisions God would make. Of course, when Adam and Eve failed to obey God, they destroyed our ability as men and women to rightly reflect God's glory, and they brought all of humanity under God's judgment. It took the Son of God, Jesus Christ, to show us again what God is really like and how he wants us to act.

There is an old suggestion that, when we have a tough choice to make, we ask ourselves, "What would Jesus do?" Surely this is the right mindset. Jesus is the perfect embodiment of God. When we act like Jesus, we act like God and we accomplish his purposes for our lives. Jesus in fact said to his disciples, "As the Father has sent me, so I am sending you" (Jn 20:21). This is a very tough assignment, as Jesus himself knew, for he warned his disciples that they could expect the same treatment that he received. Living the Christlike life is leading a cruciform life, a life lived in the face of the cross.

The profound and life-changing teaching of Jesus on the kingdom of God as we read it in the Gospels gives the shape to the life we are to lead. As we develop the notion of our purpose as human beings, we encroach upon the answer to world-view question 6 (How do we know what is right and wrong?) and so we will postpone further discussion of this topic until chapter seven.

Damaged Goods: The Peculiar Nature of Human Nature

We have touched on the issue several times above. It is time to look at it directly. Something is wrong with us as human beings. We are not what we were created to be. We are damaged goods.

Everyone agrees, of course, that something is wrong with human-kind. The world screams out to us that this is so. The question is, however, just what is it? Are we simply ignorant, needing the work of scientists to discover truth and education to bring the masses up to par? Are we incompletely evolved, needing more time and maybe some genetic engineering to bring us to biological and thus moral perfection—to work out the ape and tiger in us? Are we twisted in our thinking, needing the quiet meditation techniques of advanced human beings to set us on an inward path to spiritual tranquility where we finally realize that we have been perfect gods all along or are headed in that direction?

The Bible says no to all these suggestions. Its picture is radically different. Genesis 3 says that what went wrong with humanity is that long ago our Grand Parents, Adam and Eve, rebelled against God. Created good (Gen 1:31), they exercised the freedom they were given as God's creatures and said no to God. Tempted by the serpent (which the New Testament identifies as Satan), they ate the fruit they were commanded not to eat. Believing the serpent rather than God, they thought the fruit would make them gods themselves. The result was a broken relationship with God, with each other, with nature and with themselves. In other words, the result was spiritual, social, ecological and psychological alienation. So God removed them from the garden designed for them, symbolically showing their profound estrangement.

Humanity fallen—that is our state today. Bad news indeed!

The Good News about the Bad News

But God has not left us without hope. Already in the garden, he clothed Adam and Eve with skins of animals, symbolizing the sacrifice he would himself later pay by the death of his Son on the cross. Then beginning with Abraham, whom God called to leave his home in Ur of the Chaldees, God set in motion a scheme to bring his special creation back into good relationship with himself. He chose the seed of Abraham, the Hebrew people, to be the vehicle of his message to all humanity, giving them the Law through Moses, making of them a nation through Saul and David, constantly reminding them of their calling through the prophets, and then entering the world directly in the person of the God-man Jesus.

It is through Jesus' death on the cross that the great gulf of our alienation from God has been bridged. Because of his death and resurrection, we can be restored to right relationship with God. As the Holy Spirit works in our lives, our characters are brought more into conformity with the original image of God in us. As the apostle Paul says, "We, who with unveiled faces all reflect the Lord's glory, are being transformed into his likeness with ever-increasing glory, which comes from the Lord, who is the Spirit" (2 Cor 3:18).

This process is, however, only for those who align themselves with Jesus. "God so loved the world," the apostle John writes, "that he gave his one and only Son, that whoever believes in him shall not perish but have eternal life" (Jn 3:16). Salvation and sanctification are not automatic. Belief (and this implies an active following of Jesus as Lord, as we will see in chapter six) is required: "Whoever believes in him is not condemned, but whoever does not believe stands condemned already because he has not believed in the name of God's one and only Son" (Jn 3:18).

The whole scheme of human life, then, can be summed up in four terms: *creation, fall, redemption, glorification.* We were created good; we fell from our close relation with God; we have been redeemed by Christ; we are being glorified by the Holy Spirit. Glorification is, however, not complete this side of glory itself. And that brings us to the next world-view question.

Death: The Ultimate Test

Question 4: What happens to a person at death?

The fourth world-view question is really a subdivision of Question 3. What we believe it means to be human must contain a view of death. But it is helpful to single out this issue because it has a powerful way of concentrating the attention.

Samuel Johnson on hearing that David Hume was "no more uneasy to think he should *not be* after his life, than that he *had not been* before he began to exist," replied,

Sir, if he really thinks so, his perceptions are disturbed; he is mad; if he does not think so, he lies. He may tell you he holds his finger in the flame of a candle, without feeling pain; would you believe him? When he dies, he at least gives up all he has.[17]

Indeed, one's view of death puts to the test one's view of life. If, for example, you are a naturalist, holding that there is no supernatural realm, no spiritual substratum, then death necessarily involves the extinction of your own personality. You will be gone when your particular physical life system fails to function. If, in the face of this implication, you can be resolute in your view of human life, then you can legitimately call yourself a naturalist.

Here is where many naturalists have difficulty. They know their views lead to seeing death as the end of all personal and individual life, but the pressure to find relief is so great they either suppress their thoughts and attendant worries or they imagine a way out. The current interest in reincarnation, I think, is fueled by the fear of death and the desire for continued existence. But reincarnation implies a substratum of spirit or soul, something nonmaterial. So having begun to believe in or at least hope for reincarnation, they go on to consider the possibility that a spiritual realm exists. Surely, the whole current New Age phenomenon is in part a result of modern naturalists becoming self-consciously dissatisfied with the implications of their naturalism on just this issue. Modern pantheism, then, becomes the natural child of modern naturalism.

We see it, at least in primitive form, in the ruminations of medical scientist Lewis Thomas. In noting the intimate connection of death and life in the biosphere (one organism's life is predicated on another's death), Thomas muses:

> I find myself surprised by the thought that dying is an all-right thing to do, but perhaps it should not surprise. It is, after all, the most ancient and fundamental of biologic functions. . . .
>
> But . . . there is still that permanent vanishing of consciousness to be accounted for. . . . Where on earth does it go? Is it stopped dead in its tracks, lost in the humus, wasted? Considering the tendency of nature to find uses for complex and intricate mechanisms, this seems to me unnatural. I prefer to think of it as somehow separated off at the filaments of its attachment, and then drawn like an easy breath back into the membrane of its origin, a fresh memory for a biospherical nervous system, but I have no data on the matter.[18]

The sense of loss—that seems to be a central idea in our fear of death.

Death as Separation

For Christians death has two dimensions, in both of which the central idea is separation. In *physical death* the soul, the central core of one's being, is separated from the body. In *spiritual death* the soul is separated from God. Adam and Eve experienced spiritual death, alienation from God—symbolized by their expulsion from the garden—before they experienced physical death.

The Christian view of death is both optimistic and pessimistic. It is pessimistic in that by the time each of us realizes what has happened (by being born in sin and by sinning as we have grown up), we are already spiritually dead. The apostle Paul confirms our own self-analysis. "All have sinned and fall short of the glory of God" (Rom 3:23). We are already "dead in [our] transgressions and sin" (Eph 2:1), already separated from God. If we physically die in this condition, we are permanently separated from God. "As man is destined to die once, and after that to face the judgment" (Heb 9:27). So in the foreground of our hope for eternal life (life with God) lies a great chasm. How can we get across?

The Christian view of death is optimistic in that God bridges the chasm. "While we were still sinners, Christ died for us" (Rom 5:8). Or as John says in the so-called gospel in a nutshell: "For God so loved the world that he gave his one and only Son, that whoever believes in him shall not perish but have eternal life" (Jn 3:16). Reversing the pattern of Adam and Eve who died spiritually before they died physically, we can become spiritually alive before our physical death. That means that at death we can have a place in heaven with God and his people.

Pictures of heaven itself are rare in Scripture (see Rev 21—22). The basic promise is not so much that we will be in a wonderful "place" but that we shall be with a wonderful God, all our sorrows will be gone, and we can get on with a more fulfilling life than we can imagine.[19]

The idea of heaven as a place and not just a "state of being" does, however, have much justification in the New Testament. Perhaps the most relevant is the fact of the resurrection of the body. Jesus was the "first fruits" of the resurrection. He was not resurrected as a ghost for the tomb was empty. Though he could pass through doors (Jn 20:26), he could also eat fish (Jn 21:11-13). Paul talked about our resurrection bodies this way:

> The body that is sown [and dies like a seed] is perishable; it is raised imperishable; it is sown in in dishonor, it is raised in glory; it is sown in weakness, it is raised in power; it is sown a natural body, it is raised a spiritual body. . . . And just as we have borne the likeness of the earthly man, so shall we bear the likeness of the man from heaven. (1 Cor 15: 42, 49)

More important than anything the resurrection tells us about heaven, however, is what it confirms about the value of each individual. Each person is unique; though each has come into being at a particular time, each of us is valuable far down into the reaches of eternity. We each are responsible for our own decisions; we do not pay for another personality's sins in a former life as in the Hindu and New Age notions of reincarnation and karma. Resurrection, in fact, stands in contrast to three very common notions: (1) existence as a disembodied soul on the Other Side (2) reincarnation, that is, rebirth into another body and (3) obliteration of the soul's individuality in unification with God. The first and second of these views appear in occult and spiritualist literature. The second and third are emphasized by Hindus and many other pantheists. But none of them squares with the notion of the resurrection.

There is one more idea we need to discuss: what happens to those who do not believe in Jesus? The Gospel of John is quite clear: "Whoever believes in him is not condemned, but whoever does not believe stands condemned already because he has not believed in the name of God's one and only Son" (Jn 3:18). We are all "dead in trespasses and sins" until we are made alive in Christ. As we saw, we only live once, we only die once; after that we face judgment (Heb 9:27). Ezekiel simply says, "The soul who sins is the one who will die" (Ez 18:4). That is, we face the future separated from God, the only one who can satisfy our longings and give us peace, the only one who can restore us to what we really are, individuals made in the image of God and designed for intimate relationship with God and his people. This is hell.

Whether the biblical notion of death turns out to be optimistic or pessimistic, therefore, depends on where each one stands. It is good news for those who see through physical death to eternal life. It is bad news for those who refuse the offer of salvation in Christ. In short, for each person physical death is either the gate to life with God and his people or the gate to eternal separation from God who alone can ultimately fulfill human aspirations.

The Riddle of the World

Throughout the ages, people have wondered who they really are. There is both a glory and wretchedness about the human condition. In one of his typically gloomy moods, Hamlet says,

> What a piece of work is man! How noble in reason! How infinite in faculty! In form and moving how express and admirable! In action how like an angel! In apprehension how like a god! The beauty of the world! The paragon of animals! And yet, to me, what is this quintessence of dust? Man delights me not—no, nor woman neither.[20]

For Hamlet the problem seems less with human beings in general than with Hamlet himself. His problem is his attitude.

Blaise Pascal, the seventeenth-century philosopher, was both more realistic and more hopeful. He made the riddle generic and he suggested a solution:

> What a chimera then is man! What a novelty! What a monster, what a chaos, what a contradiction, what a prodigy! Judge of all things, imbecile worm of the earth; depository of truth, a sink of uncertainty and error; the pride and refuse of the universe!

As he drafted these lines of bitterness and gloom, he mused:

> Who will unravel this tangle? . . .
>
> Know then, proud man, what a paradox you are to yourself. Humble yourself, weak reason; be silent, foolish nature; learn that man infinitely transcends man, and learn from your Master your true condition, of which you are ignorant. Hear God.[21]

Pascal raises the great modern question: Who will unravel the tangle of man? Who will solve the riddle? And when we think we have begun to solve the riddle, what confidence can we have in our solution?

Pascal suggests that our only answer lies in listening to God. That is indeed the beginning of an answer to world-view question 5, to which we now turn.

How can I tell you why I am so or why I am not so?
Once I, Chuang Chou, dreamed that I was a butterfly
and was happy as a butterfly. I was conscious that I was
quite pleased with myself, but I did not know that I was
Chou. Suddenly I awoke, and there I was, visibly Chou.
I do not know if it was Chou dreaming that he was a
butterfly or the butterfly dreaming it was Chou.

Chuang Chou[1]

There is always more to knowing than human knowing
will ever know.

Os Guinness[2]

Chapter 5
The Christian Mind as Mind: Naming the Elephant

*T*he modern world is filled with skeptics. Make a clear statement about almost anything except your own private feelings, and you get asked, "How do you know that? Are you sure? Give me some proof." If someone asks you enough of these questions in a row, you may end up doubting whether you can really know anything at all.

Take the boy and his father whom we met in chapter three. Let's say the conversation went like this?

"Dad, what holds the world up?"

"Well, Son, it's sustained in position by gravity."

"How do you know that, Dad?"

"It's what the scientists say. Newton figured it all out a few hundred years ago."

"How do you know he was right, Dad?"

"Well, everyone today who has looked into the matter says that's the way it is. Or at least something like it. Actually, Einstein found a better way of expressing it. But only those who have studied physics more than I have can understand him."

"Why do you trust what scientists say, Dad? How do they know? Why do they trust the workings of their minds?"

Even if the father could explain the scientific method used in justifying the formulation of Newton's law of gravity, there would always be the son's question: Why, Dad?

Eventually, the father would reach his Elephant all the way down; he would simply have to say, "I'm sorry, Son. I can't do any better than that. There are some things that have to be accepted. We can't get beneath them. The simple fact of knowledge seems to be one of them: We know because we know. That is just the way it is."

The ancient Chinese philosopher Chuang Chou (who lived between 399 and 295 B.C.) faced the same dilemma. He dreamed he was a butterfly, and when he woke up he couldn't tell whether he was a butterfly dreaming he was Chou or Chou dreaming he was a butterfly.

Here then is the way this world-view issue is best formulated.

Question 5: How can anyone know anything at all?

Ground Zero

The point is this: to think, we need a starting place, a place to stand, a ground zero.

Let's say we want to go to New York. To get there we need to know not only where New York is but where we ourselves are, and there needs to lie between us and New York some medium—earth, air, water, ice—by which we can traverse the distance. So too with our thoughts. In order for our thinking to get anywhere, we need to know where we are and where we want to go, and we need some way to get there.

Ground zero is my term for where we are when we begin to think. Ground zero is terra firma, a rock which doesn't shift but stays put as we sally forth to other ground, other places. If our ground zero shifts, our perception of everything else shifts too. So the shape and position of ground zero is of ultimate importance.

For *naturalists*, ground zero has to be established within the confines of the finite human frame. There is nothing outside the human that can undergird rationality, for nothing outside the human mind thinks with anywhere nearly as much sophistication. This is not to say that nothing outside the human mind is highly complex, only that there is no indication that any other than human beings are self-conscious about their thinking. Without self-consciousness, there can be no rationality. So it is up to us as human beings to ground our own rationality. But this we cannot do with any degree of assurance.

For the naturalist, Chuang Chou's riddle is insolvable. The methods of science are of no use. Every piece of information could be a part of an illusion; every thought about it could be a part of a dream. Each individual is caught in his or her own subjectivity. The result is either arrogance or despair—the arrogance of each self in announcing the certitude of its own ruminations or the despair of each self of ever getting beyond self-doubt.[3]

For *pantheists*, ground zero is the subjective self. It makes no difference whether Chuang Chou is a butterfly dreaming he is a man or a man puzzling over the dream of being a butterfly. The riddle need not be solved, for it makes no difference which is the case. All perception is self-perception; reality is what one perceives. Modern scholar Wing-Tsit Chan, commenting on Chuang Chou's dilemma, says, "A beautiful story in itself, it is a complete rejection of the distinction between subject and object and between reality and unreality."[4] Chuang Chou himself argues that there is no ultimate distinction between this and that, including between right and wrong.[5] The Hindu phrase "Atman is Brahman" (see pp. 45 above) reflects the same view. No wonder science did not develop within a culture undergirded by pantheism—either China or India. Science is predicated on very careful distinctions.

What, then, is ground zero for a Christian, especially with respect to knowledge—one's knowledge of God, of oneself, of the world around us?

The Limits of Human Knowledge

When we come to consciousness as human beings, we do so in a social context. Our parents have raised us. We have grown up in a situation where values of a very specific kind were assumed. We learned that certain things were right or expected of us and other things were wrong. There are so many, many of these little details of lifestyle and mental attitude that we can't begin to enumerate them. By the time we begin to ask ourselves whether these little things we have learned are true or really valuable, we are doing so with mental equipment that is molded into a shape we are quite unable to detect without serious self-reflection.

In other words, by the time we come to ask what ground zero is for us—what basis our knowledge and thinking has—we are doing so with culture-shaped equipment. I, for example, do so in English (not Japanese), in twentieth-century American terms (not medieval European ones), from a unique life history like no one else's.

So how do I know that what I know has any validity, any truth, outside the context of twentieth-century America? No one in the final analysis is in any better position than I. Would what any of us knows about anything—God, ourselves, others, the world around us—be so for anyone else but ourselves?

What if another ego (another self) should crawl into my mind? What if you crawled into it. Would you recognize my mental terrain? How much of it? Would you see my knowledge of mathematics to be the same as yours? (Actually, that might be the only thing you could transfer directly to your own mind and not perceive as somewhat alien.) What about my knowledge of *Hamlet?* or of Freudian psychology? or of your parents? or of your husband or wife? or of you? or—perish the thought—of myself? What would you think of that last bit of my mental geography?

But let's get out of my mind. Who knows what we might find behind a rock or a closed door? The point I am trying to make is that none of us begins to ask the question about our own ground zero from the standpoint of an assured ground zero. To ask the question is to raise the possibility that the place where we are standing may belong only to us. Our ground zero may have no connection whatsoever to what is really so.

We are all in the position of Chuang Chou. Prove to yourself right now that you are not a butterfly dreaming that you have been challenged to prove to yourself that you are not a dreaming butterfly. I hesitate to stimulate thinking very far along such lines. The result could be a Chinese box of dreams within dreams within dreams, ad infinitum. What can be seen by pursuing such thought down a few corridors and around a few corners, however, is that no *proof* appears likely. One simply must assume at some point that he or she is awake and that the one—the "I"—who is awake is the real "I" and that this "I" is not being deceived when it assumes itself to be the real one.

As Samuel McCracken says, we need "a certain simple-minded set of working assumptions: that there is a reality out there, that we can perceive it, that no matter how difficult the perception, the reality is finally an external fact."[6]

Of course, all of us do assume something like "I am the real me; what I perceive (and am fairly certain about) is most likely so." And, except in our most intense and brooding self-reflective moments, we don't pay any attention to the fact that these are assumptions. They lie there undergirding all our thoughts and decisions and actions, but they do so subconsciously. Ask me, "Are you the real you?" and I will probably think you are pulling my leg or talking nonsense. Force me to take the question seriously, and I may begin a train of thought that will land me in some asylum. I may, however, be led to see the limits of thought. As Guinness puts it, "There is always more to knowing than human knowing will ever know."[7]

I may conclude that in order to know that my perception of who I am is not arbitrary, I must either be God (and thus all-knowing) or I must have a word from God.

Since I can always doubt that I am who I perceive myself to be, I can hardly be an all-knowing God, who would surely know if he knew. So I must, therefore, have a word from God if I am to have a ground for assured self-knowledge. This is precisely the conclusion that Pascal reached:

> Know then, proud man, what a paradox you are to yourself. Humble yourself, weak reason; be silent, foolish nature; learn that man infinitely transcends man, and learn from your Master your true condition, of which you are ignorant. Hear God.[8]

The Christian Scriptures claim that God has indeed spoken just such a word. The writer of the letter to the Hebrews says that God has spoken to us in many ways (through the prophets, for example) and that most recently he has "spoken" to us through Jesus Christ who is just like himself (Heb 1:1-3). Knowledge has come to us from outside us. There is a possibility, therefore, of finding that our ground zero is firmly rooted in reality—the truth of what is. We will look in detail at one passage rich in implications for our answer to how anyone can know anything at all.

In what follows I will attempt to make clear the ground zero John provided in his Gospel. It consists of four propositions that, in the picture I will draw, act like sides of a square. In the center of the square and permeating the whole square and qualifying each of the four sides is a fifth concept. These five ideas, then, provide the foundation not only for the argument of John's Gospel but also for the ability of anyone (believer or nonbeliever) to understand anything at all about reality. Put in philosophic terms, we will, then, be studying epistemology according to John.

God Exists

Ground zero for a Christian is a set of ideas that have immensely rich implications. That set of ideas or propositions is most fully expressed in John 1:1-4. John opens his Gospel with an answer to world-view question 1. He starts with the first reality of all realities—the one and only, sole and single, self-existent being—the infinite-personal God:

> In the beginning was the Word, and the Word was with God, and the Word was God. He was in the beginning with God; all things were made through him, and without him was not anything made that was made. In him was life, and the life was the light of men. (Jn 1:1-4 RSV)

Only one other book in the Bible opens in this way, and that opening must have been in John's mind: "In the beginning God created the heavens and the earth" (Gen 1:1). Both John and the writer of Genesis begin with the beginning that has no beginning—God.

No larger context could be set. This is the frame for the "big picture," the stopping place for all arguments tracing causes or origins. Everything begins with God. Without God nothing is that is. Genesis says that in the beginning God created everything, and John says that nothing was made that God did not make; everything was made by God.

For a Christian, therefore, the *first proposition* of ground zero is that *God exists*. Without God the Christian would not even exist, let alone know anything.[9]

Meaning: Intrinsic to Reality

The *second proposition* of ground zero is found most fully revealed in

John's account. John says, "In the beginning was the Word [Gk., *Logos*] . . . and the Word was God." John starts, not with God as Being, but with God as Meaning.

Among the New Testament writers only John directly associates the word *Logos* with God. *Logos* was a key term in Greek philosophy, especially among the Stoics.[10] Literally, *Logos* means "Word." In Greek thought, however, it denoted thought or reason, or the expression of thought or reason in words or speech. As Leon Morris says, "It was the all-pervading principle, the rational principle of the universe."[11] According to the Stoics, "the universe is pervaded by *Logos*, the eternal Reason. The term *Logos* gave expression to their deep conviction of the rationality of the universe."[12] John Marsh comments that the prolog sees "the *Logos* as the satisfying rational principle for understanding the universe. The word may thus be likened to the eternal purpose of God, giving meaning to the whole of existence."[13]

John does not develop his Gospel along Stoic lines, but he has chosen the word *Logos* and given it the prominence of being within God himself. This means at least this much—probably more: that God in Christ is the Meaning of everything. He is the ultimate Reason of all Being—his own being and the being of the universe.

The God in whom the *Logos* exists is very different from the Stoic impersonal, detached, abstract Absolute. For John, God as the *Logos* is personal and has become flesh, taken human form (Jn 1:14). But our stress here is that God is the *Logos*, and the *Logos* was in the beginning. And that means that Meaning (or Reason itself) was in the beginning.

So the *second proposition* of ground zero for a Christian is that *meaning is intrinsic to prime reality*.[14] Meaning is prior to creation. Meaning is eternal, absolute, divine.

Everything Has Meaning

The *third proposition* of ground zero is that *Meaning created everything that has been created and, therefore, everything that has been created has meaning.*

Think of it: could he who is Meaning itself (himself) create chaos or irrationality? Not only is Meaning eternal, it (he) is the reason for the nature and structure of the universe.

Colossians 1:15-17 reflects the same understanding: Christ "is the image of the invisible God, the firstborn over all creation. For by him all things were created: things in heaven and on earth, visible and invisible, whether thrones or powers or rulers or authorities; all things were created by him and for him. He is before all things, and in him all things hold together." (See also Heb 1:2.)

In other words, the created world does not contain its meaning on its own. Nor do scholars or scientists create meaning when they study the world. The structure of the relationship between a falling body and the earth was not invented by Newton when he formulated the law of gravity. Newton discovered a meaning that was built into the universe by Meaning himself. As Kepler said, scientists could "think God's thoughts after him," a phrase precisely capturing the implications, for the scholar, of the opening verses of John's Gospel.

Human Beings Can Know

The *fourth proposition* of ground zero is that *as human beings we can understand something about the meaning of the created world and Meaning (or God) himself because God built into us the capacity to do so.*

John says, "In him [the *Logos*] was life, and the life was the light of men" (v. 4).[15] God has made us so that we can *know,* truly know— not fabricate or guess or merely imagine—something about the created world and even about himself.

This theme is present even in the Old Testament. In Genesis 1 we read that God created human beings in his own image (Gen 1:27). Then in chapter two before the creation of Eve, we find God bringing the animals to Adam "to see what he would name them" (Gen 2:19).

Then God took the symbolizing work of his creature Adam and confirmed it: "Whatever the man called every creature, that was its name." God so made Adam that Adam himself could properly name the things God had made. So Adam thereby demonstrates one way he is like God. He can "create" names that aptly fit what is named. Human meaning can thus be true meaning because human beings work as a creation of Meaning.

And so it would continue to be, if it were not for the Fall. That is an issue we will have to deal with before we are finished. But it is not a proposition of ground zero. Ground zero is rooted in creation, not in the Fall or in redemption. The propositions of ground zero relate to the absolute truth of God, not the shifting sands of fallen humanity.

Figure 4 summarizes the four propositions of ground zero and displays them as four sides of a square.

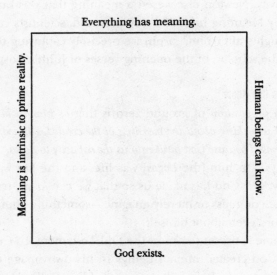

Figure 4: The components of ground zero.

Knowledge We Can More than Bank On

We now have a foundation sufficient to explain how we as human beings can know. God as Meaning made an orderly, meaningful world and made us sufficiently like himself so that our knowledge imitates his. As God is the all-knowing knower of all things, we are the sometimes-knowing knowers of some things.

But there is more to John's understanding of knowledge than is shown by these four propositions themselves. The ground zero John has laid down has an added quality.

For John, knowing has a deeply personal dimension. It is only persons who know. Computers store information; so do books. Computers reorganize that information according to programs put there by people. Books show how others have organized knowledge. But neither books nor computers know anything because neither can stand back, as it were, from the content of its knowledge and reflect on its implications. Neither can decide on its own. Books take no action. Computers react on program.

But human beings have that amazing capacity to mull things over, to imagine things not present, to reorganize their mental furniture, even to create and act on their own; no two human beings responding in the same way to any bit of knowledge or network of knowledge. Persons—those beings who are self-conscious (knowing themselves to be selves) and self-determinative (acting on their own initiative)—can manipulate data, imagine new combinations, try out fresh approaches. It is only they who know.

We in the West, however, seem to have forgotten the implications of this fact. We have inherited the notion that truth is so objective, so out-there-ish, that it stands almost forever divorced from our own selves. We react to bits of truth as if they could be moved around in our minds without ever affecting anything, especially without affecting action. To know is mental—a grasping by the mind of some external truth. Action is no necessary consequence of knowledge. To know, we take for granted, is not to do but to possess.

The mind, we seem to imagine, is like a giant bank. We move ideas in and out of various accounts. Like a bank handling other people's funds, we do business, but it is money business only. We don't actually buy anything tangible; we just handle accounts. Big minds are big banks; little minds are little banks. But since the business of banking is banking, we never require anything in particular to be done with funds.

This way of viewing knowledge as detached is characteristic especially of modern university education in both state and private schools, secular institutions and even many Christian colleges. A lecturer in French literature at Oxford University once told me that he prided himself on leaving students unaware of his own stance toward the profound spiritual and intellectual insights of Pascal. This professor, who I have reason to believe is a Christian in his own private life, remains detached, objective, distant from his academic subjects and thus transmits to his students the idea that university-level knowledge—even about such deeply spiritual topics as Pascal addresses—is not to temper one's personal life.

Let me shift the metaphor slightly. In the university we learn the rules of various games—the history game, the biology game, the sociology game, even the theology game. And we play these games like Monopoly. But we never use the money we handle in our courses to buy anything for life. The end of a semester is like the end of a Monopoly game. We pack away the play money and only take it out again when the next semester begins.

The Word Became Flesh: The Personal Nature of Knowledge

The fact that the *Logos* ("Meaning") is not an abstraction but a person means that knowledge has a deeply personal dimension. The personhood of the Logos is clear from the very first. As John says, "He was in the beginning; . . . all things were made through him. . . . In him was life" (1:2-4 RSV). The Logos is *he,* not *it.*

But most importantly, "The Logos became flesh" (1:14). Meaning himself entered his own creation, took it on, dwelt (tabernacled) with us, displaying "grace and truth." The Word of the Lord did not come to us only in words in a book, the Old Testament. He came to us in full personal (self-reflective, self-determinative) form.

William Barclay comments,

> Jesus is the expression of the mind of God. It is as if John said to the Greeks: "For the last six centuries you have been speaking about the mind of God in the universe. If you want to see what the mind of God is, look at Jesus Christ. Here, full-displayed, is that mind of God about which you have always been thinking and talking. The *logos* has become flesh. The mind of God has become a person."[16]

It is this personal character that must forever qualify our grasp of what it means to know. Truth is not complete until it is fleshed out, walks among us, interacts with us as whole persons—mind, emotions, body and will.

"I am the way and the truth and the life," the Logos says to us (14:6). "I am the bread of life" (6:35). "I am the light of the world" (8:12). "I am the resurrection and the life" (11:25).

A Logos with this character is one whose words, whose revelation of truths whether in nature or in Scripture, calls forth response. What we think places options before us. Ideas have consequences. They demand decision and call forth action. Not to know in the actual activities of daily life is not to know in the way the Bible views knowledge.

Again Genesis provides an illustration. In Genesis 2, after creating Adam, God said, "You may freely eat of every tree of the garden; but of the tree of the knowledge of good and evil you shall not eat, for in the day that you eat of it you shall die" (2:16-17 RSV). And Eve, too, knew of this command and understood it, for she repeated it to the serpent (Gen 3:1-4).

Here was the kind of knowledge that called forth a particular kind

of action. The fruit of one tree was not to be eaten. The Lord himself
had said so. But both Adam and Eve exchanged the truth of God for
the lie of the serpent. They acted on that lie and, "knowing" it in the
sense of "doing" it, they were separated from the truth, from God,
from each other, from nature and from themselves. When they acted
out of line with the true idea, they ceased to know that idea and began
to know its opposite. What consequences some ideas have!

The word *know* is used in the Old Testament to express sexual
intercourse: "And Adam knew Eve his wife, and she conceived and
bore Cain" (Gen 4:1 RSV; cf. 4:25). The most personal and intimate
of human relationships is called knowing.

It is clear, then, that each proposition of ground zero contains a
personal element: (1) God is personal, (2) the Logos is personal, (3)
creation bears the stamp of a personal Creator, (4) we as knowers are
personal. If, therefore, ground zero is a square on which we stand in
order to know anything, the area it inscribes is fully personal.

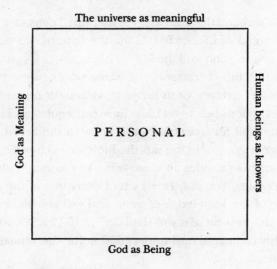

Figure 5. The personal nature of ground zero.

All Truth Is God's Truth

There is one further notion to discuss. It is not a part of ground zero, but an important implication. The idea is this: There is a continuity between the Meaning of God in Jesus and the meaning of the world truly understood by people.

The *Logos* made the world. The *Logos* became flesh. When we understand who God is in Jesus Christ, we are not doing something essentially different from understanding what water is as a chemical substance.

This must not be misunderstood. I am not saying that the *content* of the knowledge is the same. Obviously they are different. I am not saying the *way one comes to understand* the two different contents is the same. We learn who God is by God's illuminating our minds to see and understand him as he reveals himself in Scripture, in nature, in the life and teaching of Jesus, and in the holy lives of his followers. We learn the chemical composition of water from a textbook in chemistry, and we can verify it by laboratory tests. Rather I am saying that the same mind knows both in the same way; my understanding as understanding is the same. There is not, I believe, a special category in the mind or soul or heart reserved for spiritual knowledge.

Why is this so? It is because the *Logos* made the world. The meaning of the external world is that which Meaning placed there. This means that theology (the "science" of God) and scholarship (the "science" of the created world) have the same basis. All truth is God's truth; it has its origin and gets its meaning from God.

Moreover, the final witness of the world, the witness of the Scriptures, the witness of the life of Christ is the same: God is there as the ultimate Meaning of everything. Consider the witness of the world: "The heavens are telling the glory of God; and the firmament proclaims his handiwork" (Ps 19:1 RSV). Consider the witness of the Scriptures: "In many and various ways God spoke to our fathers by the prophets" (Heb 1:1 RSV). Consider the witness of Jesus: "He reflects the glory of God and bears the very stamp of his nature" (Heb 1:3 RSV). The meaning of all creation is part and parcel of the Meaning of God. Thus scholarship is an act of worship, for it is an unveiling of meaning—an illuminating of what is near and dear to God himself.

Enter the Serpent

But isn't there a problem with all of this? What about the Fall? Isn't it true that Adam and Eve, in their decision to believe the lie of the serpent, separated humankind from the truth in God? And didn't Babel further confound us by confounding our language? Indeed so.

But there are two major qualifications we need to consider. First, the Fall did not obliterate human rationality; rather it twisted it so that in all our thought we are prone to error as the sparks fly upward. But even after the Fall there are more than vestiges of intelligence. John Calvin writes, "In reading profane [he means non-Christian] authors, the admirable light of truth in them should remind us, that the human mind, however much fallen and perverted from its original integrity, is still adorned and invested with admirable gifts from its Creator."[17] Then Calvin goes on to list the virtues of the pagan philosophers, rhetoricians, medical experts, mathematicians and poets, and concludes, "Therefore, since it is manifest that men whom the Scriptures term natural, are so acute and clear-sighted in the investigation of inferior things, their example should teach us how many gifts the Lord left in possession of human nature, notwithstanding of its having been despoiled of the true good."[18] We will look at this whole issue again when we discuss the natural and social sciences in chapter eight.

Second, the Bible itself records God speaking with such people as Moses, dealing with them in their fallen state as rational beings. See, for example, the dialogs in Exodus, at the burning bush and elsewhere. Obviously, the Scriptures treat humans as capable of understanding and as responsible for not understanding.

Jesus in John 5:30-47 gives three reasons (or more, depending on how you count) that appeal to the *minds* of the Hebrews for why they should accept him as the One sent from God: (1) the witness of John the Baptist, (2) the witness of the Scriptures and (3) the witness of his works. In fact, I am convinced that the whole Gospel of John is an extended *argument* for accepting Jesus as the Messiah. John 20:30-31 states John's purpose clearly: "Now Jesus did many other signs in the presence of the disciples, which are not written in this book; but these are written that you may believe that Jesus is the Christ, the Son of God, and that believing you may have life in his name" (RSV). If the human mind is not affected by reasons, why does Jesus give them?

All of this and more suggests that there remains a good deal of native intellectual ability in fallen human nature.

But there is a second line of defense for our confidence in the possibility of human knowledge. It lies in redemption and regeneration. When a person is "saved," the process of restoration back into the image of God is begun. "And we, who with unveiled faces all reflect the Lord's glory, are being transformed into his likeness with ever-increasing glory, which comes from the Lord, who is the Spirit" (2 Cor 3:18). Our minds are being renewed as well. Paul charges us, "Do not lie to each other, since you have taken off your old self with its practices and have put on the new self, which is being renewed in knowledge in the image of its Creator" (Col 3:9-10).

So Christians, especially, can begin to realize their gradual transformation (restoration) into the image of God again. And this means they can have a growing confidence that their minds will not always play them false. God is all-knowing; we were made in his image; we are fallen; we are being restored into his image. We are not dreaming butterflies. We are human beings, puzzling over Chuang Chou's puzzle, solving it as only Christian theists can do. Of course, human knowledge is possible!

What we do with what we know is what Christian
knowing is all about.

Os Guinness[1]

Every action is the bearer and expression of more or
less theory-laden beliefs and concepts; every piece of
theorizing and every expression of belief is a political
and moral action.

Alasdair MacIntyre[2]

Chapter 6
The Discipleship
of the Mind:
Knowing and Doing

We took our clue from Pascal in the previous chapter. He suggested that if we are to solve the riddle of human existence we should "hear God." That's good advice, for, as we saw, God is the one who speaks to us both directly in his written Word and in the Word become flesh (both aspects of what theologians call special revelation) and indirectly in his created order, the world made by the Word (general revelation). Listen to God. That is a clue we will now pursue further.

This chapter forms a bridge between world-view questions 5 and 6. In the Christian world view how we know is intimately related to how we ought to act. That is, knowledge is so tied to ethics that on the most important issues of life knowing the good and doing the good are one and the same.

The divorce between knowing the good and doing it is one of the legacies of the Fall, but it has been especially obvious in twentieth-century Western culture. We know the destructive power of modern weapons, yet we continue to build them and ready them for use (which we say we will not do, at least first). University studies are ivory-tower affairs. When we study French literature, we learn about Pascal, but we never ask, Is what Pascal says true? And if so, how should I then act? What responsibility do I carry for my knowledge?

In a fully Christian world view those questions are vital. Knowledge in a biblical frame is very different from mere information. Indeed, the discipleship of the mind has two dimensions. The first is *logical;* we are to follow up on the logical consequences of those things we say we "know," seeing what is implied by what we already realize is true. The second is *behavioral;* we are to act on what we "know." Unless we do both, we do not know in the sense required by the Bible, and thus in the sense required by the Christian mind.

The Responsibility of Knowledge

The theme of knowing and doing—what Os Guinness calls the responsibility of knowledge—is central to Christian faith. I know no better way of getting to this issue, however, than to pursue it in two sections from the Gospel of John. The theme of knowledge (and its attendant term *belief*) permeates the entire Gospel. Peter says to Jesus, "We have believed, and come to know, that you are the Holy One of God" (Jn 6:69, RSV).

The first text we will examine is John 4:43-54. This passage describes an event which John places early in Jesus' ministry. Jesus has just spoken at length with the Samaritan woman at the well in Sychar. John tells the story this way:

Jesus is in Cana. Fifteen or so miles away on the Sea of Galilee is Capernaum where an official's son lies ill. The official has heard that Jesus is in the area and he believes that if Jesus will come to his home, his son can be healed. Jesus is his last best hope.

We don't know how much he has heard of Jesus' healings. But we know that the official believes enough to act on his belief. He is certain (we might say he thinks he knows) that Jesus has the power to heal his son. So with great concern and even anguish, we may imagine, he "begs" (v. 47) Jesus to come *down* from Cana to Capernaum. His son is at the point of death. Any delay will be tragic.

Now catch the tone of Jesus' response. Jesus says, in effect, "Oh, I know your kind. You are looking for parlor tricks—signs and wonders. You are not serious in your belief. You need a magic show to establish your faith in me" (v. 48).

But the man is adamant. He will not be put off. I must say here that I have great sympathy for the man from Capernaum. I know a family who have a son who a few years ago was desperately ill psychologically and spiritually. They were at wits end, hanging by the fragile fingers of their faith, endlessly praying that God would heal their son. This went on for years.

Then after an especially intense time of prayer and conflict—about five months—God turned him around. He is now gloriously clothed and in his right mind.

I know what that official must have been thinking when Jesus challenged him. And I can see myself in his position crying out in anguish: "Sir, come down before my child dies!" (v. 49). He is saying, in effect, "Sir, I'm deadly serious. You can heal my son. Please come. I don't care about myself. Heal him."

Then Jesus does something which must have stunned him. Jesus says, "You may go. Your son will live" (v. 50).

Do you see in what position that put the official? What is he to do? If he says, "Oh no, Jesus, you've misunderstood. Please come to my home where I know you can heal," he will be doing exactly what Jesus has accused him of. He will not be truly believing Jesus. Jesus could then simply say, "You see, I told you so. You believe in my power of healing when I'm present with a person in need, but you do not believe in me. I have told you that your son is healed. But you do not believe me."

What a dilemma! If he continues to beg, he puts his faith in Jesus in jeopardy; if he returns to Capernaum without Jesus, he runs the risk of losing his son.

Jesus has forced a choice: (1) to believe in Jesus and all Jesus is and claims to be, including Jesus' unsubstantiated statement that his son is healed, or (2) to reject Jesus whom he sees as his only hope.

But the man believes Jesus. He puts his faith into action, and gloriously his belief in Jesus and Jesus' word of assurance is confirmed. On the way home his servants meet him with the good news. "Your son is healed," they say.

"When," the man asks, and he learns that the turning point of his son's illness was the very hour Jesus spoke his healing word.

Then John says something very interesting. When the man learned of his son's recovery, "he and all his household believed" (v. 53).

Didn't he believe already? Of course he did. He proved it by his action. From the time given for the healing, some commentators believe the man spent a night in Cana before returning. In any case, now his belief has been confirmed. He knows—has justified belief—that Jesus is trustworthy.

His "household," on the other hand, is now just beginning its trek from belief to knowledge. For the man from Capernaum and his family the earlier words of the Gospel of John have become worked out in everyday life: "The Word became flesh and dwelt among us, full of grace and truth; we have beheld his glory, glory as of the only Son from the Father" (1:14).

Knowledge and Belief

This text is a rich paradigm of biblical epistemology. From it we can draw five important aspects of what it means to know. The first point is a challenge to the modern dichotomy between knowledge and belief, also expressed in the term "fact/value dichotomy."

Point 1: Knowledge and belief are in the same category. Both have to do with matters of truth.

A number of years ago the English department chairman at Nebraska Wesleyan University, where I was teaching, more than once stopped our conversations dead in their tracks. After a particularly intense discussion about the Christian faith, he would say, "Sire, it's okay for you to believe in Jesus, but just don't tell me that what you believe is true."

This is a typical modern response. The argument goes like this: Religious belief is just that—belief. It has nothing to do with matters of truth and falsity.⁵ One either believes or not, and it's okay for you to believe Jesus is the only way to God and for me to believe that there are other ways. The fact that these claims are contradictory is beside the point. They are belief claims, not truth claims.

Over and over I have heard this argument on campus. When a claim is made for the truth of the Christian religion, the response comes back, "It's true for you. But it doesn't have to be true for me." And sometimes this comment is continued, "Jesus is God to you, but he is not God to me. It's okay for you to believe in a particular God. Just don't be so intolerant as to try to make me believe it too."

Countering this view is very difficult. The "value" of tolerance is so ingrained on campus, that any exclusive claim is rejected before it is considered rationally.

Of course, it follows—as night follows day—that if the God of the Bible exists, he exists. Nothing we can do—believe in him or not—will change that. His existence is a fact. So is any moral orientation he may have. His goodness and what constitutes it—love, truth, grace, justice, for example—is a fact.

In the modern mindset, however, both God's existence and his character are put in the category of value. Values are personal. Each has his or her own. They came either through socialization or through considered choice or some combination. But one thing is sure: they are not set in concrete. I can change my own any time I want. I can believe in God and take the Ten Commandments as normative in my life. Or I can not believe in God. And if I don't believe in God, I can ignore any ethical norms that someone else who does believe in God may try to impose on me. So the mindset settles in to keep claims on it from the outside from being considered at all.

How did the fact/value dichotomy become so dominant in our society? Primarily it came about when the idea of a transcendent God to whom we are responsible ebbed from our cultural consciousness. Dates are impossible to give, but the process started in the Enlightenment of the eighteenth century, intensified throughout the nineteenth century and has now become all but complete.[4] In the Middle Ages and up through the Protestant Reformation, the notion that human beings were created by God to glorify him in their behavior dominated Western culture. People were to seek after God, find salvation and realize the end toward which they were created—eternal life with God and his people. In such a situation, moral precepts are a fact of existence. There is a purpose for human life: what helps the realization of that purpose is good; what does not is not good.

In the wake of the Enlightenment, and the naturalistic world view which it spawned, human beings lost their purpose. Why? Because people came to see themselves as solely the product of nondirective, nonpurposeful forces in the natural order. We are simply here and conscious of our hereness; but we have no intentional reason for being here, for we were not intended. So no particular action on our part is called for. If we were not intended, there is no reason even to continue to be.[5] We may be in the same positions as the dinosaurs—interesting (but only to human beings, by the way) products of material forces, adapted to the environment for a few million years but no longer suited for life on the planet and therefore extinct. Our catastrophic time may be coming as it came for those magnificent creatures of biospheric history.

If we are indeed the unintended product of the biosphere, then any value we put on anything will have to be based solely on human choice. But why should we choose one way of life over another? Try as we will, we will find no reason based on anything other than arbitrary choice.

Take the case of a watch. If I tell you that my watch keeps time erratically—sometimes it's fast, sometimes slow, sometimes stops entirely, then starts again—we all know that I have a bad watch. It is not doing what it is intended for—keeping time. We created the watch. We know what it's for. Our judgments about it, therefore, are matters of fact. If I tell you that on my farm the land is eroding and the crops are decreasing each year, but that on the farm next to mine on similar terrain the land is holding and the crops are increasing, you could say that I was a poor farmer and my neighbor a good one. We as human beings created farming. We know what farmers are for.

But what are we for—we human beings? We did not make ourselves. We found ourselves already made—made by a concatenation of forces that had nothing in mind at all, for these forces had no mind at all. What is the purpose of the culture which values farmers? Why should it value them? In a naturalistic world, all answers to these questions are merely "values." They are not "facts." And when we value different things in different ways, finding ourselves fighting over all manner of matters—from toys to countries—we have no basis for arbitrating disputes.

As our culture becomes increasingly pluralistic, more and more matters get put in the category of "value," and more and more difficulties arise in getting along with each other. The legacy of the fact/value dichotomy is growing social chaos.

Lesslie Newbigin ponders our plight, wondering what if—what if the Christians have had it right all along?

What if it were simply a fact that the one by whose will and purpose all things exist, from the galactic system to the electrons and neutrons, has acted and spoken in certain specific events and words in order to reveal and effect his purpose and to call us to respond in love and obedience?[6]

The answer is obvious. It would make all the difference in the world. Moral judgments would be judgments about facts. There would be no fact/value dichotomy. What's true would be true—not just a matter of opinion or belief, but a matter of knowledge. What's true for you, if true, would be true for me. We might disagree, but we would have a genuine substantial disagreement, not just a tiff over taste. The real question, as one student at Valparaiso University put it, is not "Do I believe in God?" but rather "Does God believe in me?"

This is just the kind of view we meet in the Gospel of John. Take the passage at hand. The official's son was either healed or he was not. Jesus did not tell the man, "I'm glad you believe in me. Your son is healed—not in quite the way you want (actually he has already died)—he is healed in your 'heart.' You can now deal emotionally with the loss of your son."

Indeed, a religious claim—Jesus' claim that the boy is healed—is either true or false. And this is the case with every claim in Scripture from "Jesus died on the cross" to "God was reconciling the world to himself in Christ" (2 Cor 5:19). Some are is subject to historical evidence; some are not. But both kinds are either true or false.

Justified True Belief

There is a second aspect of knowledge to be drawn from the story of the healing of the official's son.

Point 2: Knowledge is justified, true belief.

This definition of knowledge is actually one formulated by some modern philosophers, including some Christian philosophers.[7] But the point is well made in the text we have been reading.

The official believed that Jesus could heal if he came to his home. He had, it would seem, heard reports of Jesus' activity elsewhere, and he trusted those reports enough to travel the fifteen or so miles up rough hilly roads to Cana.

Jesus asks him to do more, however. He asks him to believe him when he says his son is healed. The man does. His faith, then, is not left dangling. It is confirmed in the world of space and time—not the world of airy-fairy superspirituality, but the ordinary world of flesh and blood, of dirty dishes, of economic recession, of midterms and final exams. In other words, the man's *belief* in Jesus was *justified*. What he believed was true. It is just this "justified, true belief" that constitutes knowledge.

In this complex world we live in, such rock-hard knowledge is not always easy to come by. We can tell when it's raining outside rather easily. We can learn to get along rather well—with lots of effort—even in an academic environment where much is required of us whether we are students or professors. But much of this getting along is bought at the price of accepting on authority the judgments (and I'm afraid often mere unsubstantiated opinions) of others. When it comes to having lots of knowledge (justified beliefs) about the things that really matter, we are paupers.

Is there a God? What is he or she or it like? What is life for? How should we then live? How indeed can I know anything at all?

If our beliefs could be justified in these matters, we would be of all people most blessed. That is, of course, what Christians think has happened in the life and teachings of Jesus. What we learn of him in Scripture, what we find justified after all our modern skepticism has worked on us, what we act on—this is knowledge in a biblical frame.

Progress in Knowledge

Belief and knowledge are not in a static relationship. A dynamic fuels the formula, and we can move as Christians toward greater knowledge.

Point 3: Belief and knowledge are progressive.

The man from Capernaum believed Jesus could heal if he was present with the one needing healing. He acted on this belief. Then Jesus asked the man to believe beyond the evidence already presented to him (the testimonies he had heard). The man acted on this. This belief was confirmed by the healing of his son. We can now imagine that the man was ready to believe Jesus for whatever he would tell him.

His family, however, was one step behind him. When the "household" believed, they were just starting their trek toward fuller knowledge of Jesus.

Knowledge and Obedience

If one does not move toward knowledge, even one's sheer belief is eroded.

Point 4: Progressive knowledge is predicated on obedience to belief.

There was only one way for the man from Capernaum to know if what Jesus was saying was true. He had to act on implicit faith in Jesus. He could not ask him for any more information. He could not ask him to come to Capernaum. He could only "depart" (v. 51).

So related is belief to action, that it is fair to say that if you believe, you will act. If you do not act, you show by that nonaction that you do not believe.

In fact, it is through obedience that knowledge comes. Through action comes confirmation and justification. (See figure 6.)

belief ⎯⎯► *action* ⎯⎯► *knowledge* . . . .

Figure 6. The flow of progressive belief and knowledge.

Belief in action produces knowledge. Each bit of knowledge leads one to further belief, which when acted upon is confirmed if indeed the belief is true. If one's belief is not true, then confirmation does not come.

Many of our religious beliefs may begin with risk and end with certitude and justification only after we have obeyed what looks at first to be scant evidence. Take the following as an illustration:

A mountain climber is trapped on a precipice. He can neither see to get up or down. He hears a voice saying, "Put your right foot over about a foot. You'll find a way down from there."

But the climber can't see the foothold, and to make the move, he has to leave the one sure hold he has with his left foot.

So he asks the voice, "Who are you?"

"Hans Schmidt," comes the answer.

The mountain climber has never heard of "Hans," but he knows the Schmidt family to be highly reputed mountain climbers.[8]

What should the trapped mountain climber do? He has some information about the voice. He has little choice but to wait, in which case he may remain on the mountain long past any hope of rescue, or to risk the step the voice has suggested.

Of course, if the voice is right, the man will be saved. If the voice is wrong, he will fall to his death.

Christians would say that for those of us trapped on the precipices of this world, a voice comes claiming to be from God. We have heard about this God, and we have met others who claim to know him. There is indeed a book that claims to contain his word, to even tell stories about how he himself came into the world, climbed the precipices himself, then made preparation through his own death for our salvation from the steep slopes of human existence.

If we follow out the hints readily available in the world around us, we find that the belief that this God really exists is not based on wishful thinking but is quite rational, quite reasonable. It may not be strictly provable like a mathematical formula, but it can be justified like a verdict in a court of law. When the rules of evidence are all properly in operation, a reasonable verdict can be rendered. In other words, our situation is better than that of the man trapped on the mountain side—or at worst, no worse.

The flow of confirmation, however, remains: belief through obedience to knowledge.

This flow is, of course, the ideal form. Sometimes one's actions bring about the desired state of affairs for reasons other than one's beliefs. Likewise, some beliefs on which we act may not be confirmed this side of glory, for instance, that there is indeed glory on the other side. But the paradigm is a guide to discipleship. We must act on what we say we believe (and say we know), or we really do not believe or know at all—at least not in the biblical sense.

The Dynamics of Belief and Disbelief

The Gospel of John gives many instances in which those he spoke with refused to believe even on the evidence in front of them. In John 9, for example, Jesus heals a man blind from birth. The man grows in belief and knowledge from recognizing that Jesus is the one who healed him, through thinking him a prophet and a man from God, to finally concluding that he is worthy of worship (Jn 9:11, 17, 33, 38). This takes place in the context of a challenge from the religious authorities. The man has to act on what he knows from experience (he has been healed) to what he comes to believe as he is challenged by others to identify Jesus.

There are indeed two aspects to the discipleship of the mind at this point. As I pointed out at the beginning of this chapter, one must (1) follow out the logical consequences of one's belief, asking what logically follows from what I hold to be true, and (2) act on what one says one believes. This is precisely what the blind man does. And he is put out of the synagogue for his effort! His following of Jesus leads to persecution; his is the way of the cross.

The religious authorities, of course, move in precisely the opposite direction. They do not believe that Jesus is capable of healing the man born blind. They refuse the evidence before their eyes, and when they leave they are in worse shape than when they came. When the Pharisees asked Jesus, "Are we blind, too," Jesus replied, "If you were blind, you would not be guilty of sin; but now that you claim that you can see, your guilt remains" (Jn 9: 40-41).

There is a further passage in the Gospel of John that illustrates yet another aspect in the movement from belief to knowledge. Two long chapters (Jn 7—8) focus on a long discourse between Jesus and the religious authorities.[9] In that section, Jesus argues that he is the one sent from God, and the authorities argue he is not. Finally, John says, "Even as he spoke, many put their faith in him." Hearing this, a reader of the Gospel may sigh and say, "It's about time!" And indeed it is.

But then, note what Jesus says next:

To the Jews who had believed him, Jesus said, "If you hold to my teaching, you are really my disciples. Then you will know the truth, and the truth will set you free." (Jn 8:31-32)

He puts those who had believed to the test. They are to "hold to [Jesus'] teaching." This is, on the one hand, an instruction for action. They are to live by the teaching of Jesus. On the other hand, it is simply an obvious corollary to their "believing him," to their acknowledging that he is the one he claims to be (at this point, the "one sent from God"). But if he is the one sent from God, then continuing to listen to him is a logical thing to do. In short, they are to (1) grasp the logical consequences of believing Jesus and (2) take appropriate action. That will make them Jesus' disciples.

So what does Jesus tell them as he continues to teach? Something very glorious and something very troubling. That they will be free is glorious. That this implies that they are not free now is troubling. So they begin to deny what Jesus says. "We are Abraham's descendants," they protest, "and have never been slaves of anyone. How can you say that we shall be set free?" (v. 33). Never mind the time in Egypt or Babylon! Never mind Israel's present relationship to Rome! they seem to say. We are free; we do not need deliverance from anything.

As the argument continues, not only do they cease to believe Jesus is the one sent from God, but they call him a Samaritan (an ethnic slur) and accuse him of being possessed by a demon. Disbelief has a dynamic too. If when presented with the truth one does not believe it, one does not remain neutral but believes a lie. Believing a lie has consequences. As Adam and Eve believed the Lie of the serpent and lost their intimate relationship with God, so the religious leaders in this passage of John move so far away from Jesus that they take up stones to stone him (v. 59).

Trust and Obey

Knowing Jesus involves more than believing what he says. It means knowing *him* as a person.

Point 5: Knowledge of Jesus involves trust in him and in his word.

We all face the Master just as the official did from Capernaum. Over and over as I read Scripture in search of truth—even the truth about epistemology—God speaks to me as he did to the official. He says, "Sire, you just look to me to answer your intellectual questions on your terms."

And I have to respond, "Lord, come down before my child dies. To whom can I go? You—you alone are the Word of Truth. I cannot live without you."

Then he says to me, "If you love me, you will obey what I command. And I will ask the Father, and he will give you another Counselor to be with you forever—the Spirit of truth" (Jn 14:15).

Jesus wanted the man from Capernaum to believe him, not simply to believe he could heal, but to believe *him*. That means believing everything he says. And that, as we have seen, means acting on what he says, obeying his words. It means getting to know him as a person

THE DISCIPLESHIP OF THE MIND: KNOWING AND DOING

and not just as a "teacher" or "command giver." Getting to know Jesus is in its briefest form the path of Christian living.

Doing in Order to Know

What happens when these principles are applied today? I want to recount a story that captures the essence better than any other I have ever heard. It comes from Rebecca Manley Pippert, who at the time this story took place was a campus staff member with InterVarsity Christian Fellowship.[10]

One day a student, whom Pippert calls Sue, sought her counsel. Her best friend, Larry, had become a Christian but she was not a believer. She knew the basics of the Christian gospel, she even thought the Christians she had met were pretty good folk, but she was not convinced it was all true. So she asked for help.

Pippert told her to "tell God (or the four walls)" that she wanted to know if Jesus is God and that if she knew, she would follow him. Sue was to read the Gospels each day, find something that made special sense and then do it when the opportunity arose.

So Sue did this, having what she called her "pagan quiet times." Later she told Pippert that Jesus' words in the Sermon on the Mount "hit her between the eyes": "If someone steals your coat, don't let him have only that but offer your cloak as well." So she prayed, "Listen, walls—or God if you're there—I'm trying to do what this verse says. . . . I'm trying to do things your way in order to find out if you exist and if Jesus really is who he says. Amen."

The day began and Sue says she forgot about the verse until a long and almost violent argument broke out between her and a young man who wanted to take over her thesis study desk at the library. As the argument heated up, the other student blurted out, "Look. I'm stealing it from you whether you like it or not."

Suddenly it hit her.

I just looked at him and moaned, "OHHHHH, no. No. I can't

believe it." And to myself I thought, "Look God, if you're there, I do want to know if Jesus is God. But isn't there some way of finding out besides obeying that verse? I mean, couldn't I tithe or get baptized or give up something else? But DON'T TAKE MY THESIS DESK! I mean with my luck, I'll give up the desk and then discover you don't exist."

But Sue began to realize that here was her opportunity to live by Jesus' standards. So with some reluctance she "took a deep breath, tried not to swear and said, 'OK, you can have the desk.' " But a librarian had overheard the argument and was outraged about the young man's demand. So there ensued a long series of dialogs with the university authorities, none of whom wanted to make a decision about who would get the desk. Finally, the last person they talked with asked, "Well, what does Sue think we should do?"

Sue quickly reflected on what she was learning about Jesus from the Bible and her friend Larry whose life she had seen changed for the better. She felt drawn to Jesus. And finally she simply said he could have the desk. When the boy asked why she had given in, she simply said, "Hey, if there's one thing I've learned from reading about Jesus and meeting some real Christians, it's that Jesus would give you a whole lot more than a thesis desk if you'd let him. I know Jesus would give it to you. So that thesis desk is yours."

Her next remarks make my point. She told Pippert, "As I said those words, I just simply *knew* it was all true. I kinda felt like God was saying, 'Well done. That's the way I want my children to behave.' "

Belief for Sue was primitive. She didn't believe much about Jesus before she began to "hold to" his teaching (Jn 8:32). But she obeyed fully in a situation which cost her. To be a disciple required sacrifice. But in the sacrifice itself came what she had been searching for—a sense of confidence that Jesus was the one sent from God, the one in whom life finally made sense.

There is a point to be made as well about the kind of knowledge

Sue came to have. She was interested in knowing whether Jesus was who he claimed to be—a matter of metaphysical (or ontological) fact. She found confidence to say he was by virtue of the sense of rightness that followed her obeying his moral precepts. There is a consistency to God's world. Ethical matters relate to metaphysical matters. There is no fact/value dichotomy. Ethical norms are moral facts, just as physical states are facts.

The Pattern of Discipleship

The pattern we saw in John's story of the man from Capernaum is repeated in Sue's story. It is a pattern that is universal and should begin to guide our action as disciples.

1. Something hits us as true.
   a. that Jesus can heal if he comes to our home.
   b. that the principle of giving your cloak (without anger) to one who demands it of you is a valid, high moral principle.
2. An occasion arises where our belief is tested by a chance to apply the principle.
3. We obey.
4. We have confirmed in some way the principle of truth we have acted on.

There is indeed a direct relationship between believing and knowing. We come to know what we believe when we put our beliefs into action and find them confirmed. Knowing and doing are part and parcel of each other. If we know, we do. If we do not do, we do not know; in fact, we do not even believe.

If then knowing means doing, what should we know and do? The answer, of course, is that we should know and do the good. And that leads to the next chapter.

We bring good things to life.

General Electric Television Commercial

He passed his fingers along a steel rib and felt the stream of life that flowed in it; the metal did not vibrate, yet it was alive. The Engine's five-hundred horse-power bred in its texture a very gentle current, fraying its ice-cold rind into a velvety bloom. Once again the pilot in full flight experienced neither giddiness nor any thrill; only the mystery of metal turned to living flesh.

Saint-Exupéry[1]

Chapter 7
Getting to Know the Good: Bringing Good Things to Life

A few years ago a car displaying two bumper stickers was seen leaving the parking lot of the Graduate Theological Union library in Berkeley, California. One sticker read, "Save the Baby Seals," and the other, "A Woman Has Absolute Rights over Her Own Body."

Animal rights elevated over human rights, religious freedom proscribed by law, apartheid justified by theology, infinite moral options promoted by limitless tolerance, a church silent on all but the issues of private morality or highly selective in its choice of social issues to engage. Moral confusion: this is our world—at least in North America and Europe.

As Christians we have not kept pace with society. Once at the forefront of moral discourse, we have nothing to say on many key issues of our day. What shall we think of animal rights? When does building a dam infringe on the rights of the environment or of the people affected immediately and in the long run? Should we preserve all threatened forms of biological life? At what cost? And to whom? These and a host of other questions should burst any bubble of ethical self-confidence we may think we have as Christians.

We cannot answer all these questions in this chapter. We can only begin to survey the land we have to conquer. From where we stand on the east bank of the river Jordan the land looks full of giants. We will select only one to challenge, if not slay. But let us first look closer at the whole scene through the lens of a Christian world view and address forthrightly the sixth world-view question.

Question 6: How do we know what is right and wrong?

A Basis for Ethics

We saw in chapters five and six some of the reasons that people disagree on key issues. In our Western culture, *naturalism* has triggered a dichotomy between facts and values. Facts are public; they include anything one can identify, measure and submit to a scientific method of analysis. Values, on the other hand, are private; they are freely chosen by anyone who wants to so choose. Ironically, since naturalists hold that there is no ethical realm apart from human thought, intuition or choice, they have no choice to think otherwise.

Pantheism, on the other hand, ultimately avoids the problem altogether by seeing it as an issue applying only to this world of illusory distinctions. In the final analysis, Chuang Chou said, "There is no distinction between 'this' [right] and 'that' [wrong]."[2] And modern pantheist Shirley MacLaine echoes this, as she quotes her own Higher Self: "Until mankind realizes there is, in truth, no good and there is, in truth, no evil—there will be no peace."[3]

MacLaine does not seem to see the internal inconsistency of what her Higher Self says. If there is no distinction between good and evil, then it is just as good to be wrong about one's thoughts as to be right about them, that is, just as good to have false thoughts as true ones. That means anything she or we or anyone believes is equally good or evil. Why should she tell us this and we believe it? All impetus to knowledge is undermined. Moreover, MacLaine seems to want peace more than nonpeace. But if there is no difference between good and evil, why prefer one over the other? MacLaine illustrates the fact/value dichotomy with a vengeance. Values are anything any one of us chooses. MacLaine chooses peace. But she has no basis for encouraging anyone else to do the same thing.

Christian theism, however, does have ethical norms. These norms are predicated on the existence of an infinite-personal God who is good.

God is good. This is the prime revelation about God's character. From it flow all others. To be good means to *be* good. God *is* goodness. That is, *what* he is is good. There is no sense in which goodness surpasses God or God surpasses goodness. As being is the essence of his nature, goodness is the essence of his character. Goodness is therefore a fact about the way things are. Goodness has, in philosophic terms, an ontological status.

God's goodness is expressed in two major ways, through holiness and through love. Holiness emphasizes his absolute righteousness which brooks no shadow of evil. As the apostle John says, "God is light and in him is no darkness at all" (1 Jn 1:5 RSV). God's holiness is his separateness from all that smacks of evil. But God's goodness is also expressed as love. In fact, John says "God is love" (1 Jn 4:16), and this leads God to self-sacrifice and the full extension of his favor to his people, called in the Hebrew Scriptures the "sheep of his pasture" (Ps 103:3).

God's goodness means, then, that there is an absolute standard of righteousness found in God's character. So what does it mean for a human being to be good? Since we are made in the image of God, for us to be good means for us to be like God in his goodness. Functionally, to be good is to be and do what we are made to be and do.

Let's recall a few simple examples.[4] As we saw in chapter six, a good watch keeps accurate time. A good farmer raises plentiful crops and keeps the land fertile. A good air conditioner would keep my room cool while I write this book during a hot summer in Chicago and actually has as I have revised it.

So then what is a good person? Naturalists can not answer this question because they do not know what human beings are for. We arose from the biological soup, not by design or purpose, but by a combination of accident and the inevitable execution of the essential orderliness of the cosmos—chance and determinism, says Jacques Monod.[5] But Christians do know what human beings are for.

Made in God's image, Adam and Eve were themselves created good (Gen 1:31); they had a moral capacity built into them; they reflected the goodness of God's character. Moreover, they were given the ability to stay good, growing in knowledge, through obedience. But their good natures could be changed by disobedience.

Adam and Eve were created for a purpose—to multiply and fill the earth, to cultivate the garden, to have dominion over the rest of the created order and thereby to glorify God. A good person, therefore, is one who glorifies God.

We cannot deal with all the ways we can seek to glorify God in our actions. Some of them—especially issues in private morality—have been dealt with over and over. Do we need another discussion of God's view of premarital sex? Maybe not for another fifty years! A few social issues—like abortion and world hunger—are being treated well already. So, as an illustration of how to go about getting to know the good, I have chosen to focus on an issue that is receiving little attention by Christians. Technology, a seemingly benign topic, ought to raise many more serious questions for us than it has. Getting to know the good in relation to technology may be more complex than we at first imagine.

Technology: One Giant in the Land

There is nothing more pervasive in the modern world than technology. Ours is an age not just of highly complex machines—automobiles, stealth bombers and computers—but of machinelike organizations, machinelike therapies and machinelike thinking. So much does technology form the context of our daily lives that we no more take it into account than a fish does the water it swims in. Its ubiquity makes it invisible. But its ubiquity also makes it a major issue. For when we begin to reflect for a moment, we soon realize that many of the problems we face as a society have a high technological dimension.

As I write this, for example, Exxon has just spent millions of dollars on a technological solution to a technological accident—the clean-up of the oil spill from a tanker that went aground in Valdez Bay in Alaska. Oil prices have already responded by rising. The human error of a drunken ship captain has combined with the inevitability of crude oil chemistry, marine biology and ocean currents to give us one of the worst ecological disasters in this decade. But it may not be the worst. Rich oxygen-producing, tropical rain forests are being depleted each year by thousands of acres. Tons of toxic chemicals are spilling into the atmosphere as I write; these will rain back into our lakes and rivers, not only killing fish but putting harmful chemicals into the food chain.

Getting to know the good will require a response to this problem, for people make and employ the technology that sets the context for human life. Decisions about its development and deployment are not, therefore, just "technical" but include a clear ethical dimension. So how do we get started in understanding technology and getting to know the good in relation to it?

Getting Started

For a Christian the first step in getting to know the good is to have a firm grasp on the basic ethical teachings of Scripture. The Scripture forms the central core of our understanding of how we should live. As we grow as Christians we should be so exposing ourselves to God's Word, and so obeying it when we understand it, that God's perspective becomes ours. For that, nothing more special than concentration on the Bible in groups and as individuals under the leadership of the Holy Spirit is required. This is basic discipleship. There is no magic to how this is done, no short cut to ethical and spiritual maturity. It is a long, hard process that will not end till we see Jesus in all his glory and know him as we are known.

From the beginning of our study in the discipleship of the mind, we have constantly used the Bible as our authority. It is from Scripture that we learn that the fear of the Lord is the beginning of wisdom, that humility is a basic virtue, that God is the prime reality. For books on how to understand the Bible check the footnote and the bibliography (pp. 230-31) for my recommendations.[6]

One thing we learn fairly quickly when we read the Bible: it often does not answer our specific questions specifically, especially those having to do with modern life. Should we continue to build gasoline-burning engines when we now know how badly the products of its combustion pollute our environment? Should we develop high-tech systems for preserving the lives of octogenarians? or babies born without their own life-support systems? What is the best way to plan for a transportation system that will serve our world in the next century? Should I work in the field of technology? If so, what could I best be doing? The questions could be multiplied endlessly. It is obvious that we will need to understand the context of our lives by reference to sources other than the Bible.

Understanding the Issues
So how do we get a grasp on our context? Investigate, research, read, study, think, discuss: There is no substitute for concentrated effort.

But where do you start?

It depends. Where are you? What do you already know? or think you know? Move out from there.

When I became interested in the nature of technology and its problems, I knew through conversation with friends and general exposure to the media—*The New York Times Book Review,* the daily papers, books I had read before—about a few books that had been written on the topic. I started there.

Specifically, I started by reading and scanning what I already knew to be a classic study of technology—Jacques Ellul's *The Technological Society.* But what if I hadn't known about Ellul? Simple. Any major book or article on the nature of technology will eventually refer to Ellul's work. It will become obvious that he is considered a formidable figure in the field; he is either hated or admired, depending on the critic, and obviously a person whose work you will want to investigate for yourself. When you find out that he is not only a sociologist but a Christian whose position is explicitly undergirded by Scripture and theology, it becomes doubly obvious that you should check out his work.

As I read Ellul, it became clear to me that technology as he understood it is not just the accumulation of highly engineered products but an entire mindset, a way of thinking he calls *technique:* "the *totality of methods rationally arrived at and having absolute efficiency* (for a given stage of development) in *every* field of human activity."[7]

How do we normally attack a problem? Do we not carefully divide up the issues and attack them with a set procedure: (1) we do this, (2) we do that, (3) we do the next thing? Do we not aim at efficiency (in terms of time, energy and money) in all of our efforts? When we do, we are employing *technique.* But isn't this the way to solve all problems? How else would we do it? Our inability to think of any alternative is an indication of how much *technique* governs our thinking.

From Ellul I went on to other books and articles that I found by using the computer catalog of the library at the University of Delaware where I was teaching for a brief period. I also contacted a friend who sent me the textbooks used at Michigan Technological University in a course in the nature of technology, and I spoke with the professor who teaches ethics in engineering at the University of Texas. Somewhere along the way I spoke and later corresponded with a Christian professor at the University of Illinois who was himself developing an approach to the ethics of technology. He led me to the work of five other Christian scholars at the Calvin Center for Christian Scholarship. I will give the details below. Suffice it say here that this proved to be my most helpful contact.

I was able to conduct much of my search for material, therefore, by personal interviews. This is not possible for everyone. But excellent substitutes are. University libraries are widely available to both students and their surrounding communities. And public libraries are often equipped to handle interlibrary loans. I could easily have acquired access to all the material I eventually used for my own study (which by the way is not finished) without personal contact.

In a field like technology, however, little has been written from a Christian perspective. In some ways it was fortuitous that I learned about the work of the Christian professor at the University of Illinois. But bibliographies do exist that list the work of Christians in various fields. One of the best of these was prepared by Brian Walsh and Richard Middleton and appeared first in *The Transforming Vision*.[8] They have revised and updated that bibliography, and it now appears as appendix to this book. It would be an excellent place to start your search for a Christian approach, not just to technology, but to most other major issues facing our society.

To illustrate what arises when one attempts to grapple with a complex issue I will take the remainder of the chapter to describe what I learned about technology. To begin let us look at three examples of problems fostered by technology. I was not long in learning about the celebrated case of rubber tomatoes.

Case 1: Rubber Tomatoes

In the late 1940s the University of California—Davis developed a tomato harvester. This machine can "harvest tomatoes in a single pass through a row, cutting the plants from the ground, shaking the fruit loose, and (in the newest models) sorting the tomatoes electronically into large plastic gondolas that hold up to twenty-five tons of produce headed for canning factories."[9] This sounds like a good idea. The goal of efficiency is realized. But the matter does not end here.

Three unhappy effects resulted. First, in order to accommodate the harvester, the tomatoes were bred to be "hardier, sturdier and less tasty" than before. Second, thousands of farm workers were put out of a job because the pickers were more cost effective. And third, the smaller farmers could not afford the machines, and so some of them went out of business. Langdon Winner estimates that

> the number of tomato growers declined from approximately 4,000 in the early 1960s to about 600 in 1973, and yet there was a substantial increase in tons of tomatoes produced. By the late 1970s an estimated 32,000 jobs in the tomato industry had been eliminated as a direct consequence of the mechanization. Thus a jump in productivity to the benefit of very large growers has occurred at the sacrifice of other rural agricultural communities.[10]

A number of implications can be drawn from the case of the rubber tomatoes. But we will hold them until all three cases are before us.

Case 2: Chlorofluorocarbons and the Ozone Layer

Since 1972, a multinational group of scientists working for manufacturers of chlorofluorocarbons (CFCs) have been studying their effect on the ozone layer. Their work is by no means over, but at least some of the results have caused these scientists and others monitoring their work considerable concern. It appears that the ozone layer is in fact being depleted and that that will increase the level of ultraviolet radiation reaching the earth's surface. This in turn affects human health by increasing the incidence of cataracts and skin cancer (the latter especially among the white population).

One of these scientists, Dr. Linsley (Jim) Gray, a personal friend of mine, spends 25-30% of his time on the project and has flown over Greenland in a research plane with others who have been developing ways to measure the ozone depletion over the Arctic.

Gray insists that this is an honest effort by manufacturers to assess the situation, and that already there is enough evidence of the harmful effect of CFCs to put curbs on their production. The manufacturer he represents and many others are and have been working to provide substitutes for the CFCs now employed in refrigeration and numerous other industrial uses. So far this looks like a straightforward problem. Stop producing and using these chemicals and find substitutes. But the issues are not so simple.

First, there is a problem in controlling the production of CFCs. Not all the nations manufacturing the chemical have joined the already existing group of manufacturers and nations who are cutting back on the production. Some of these are Third World nations who in the short run could benefit by continuing or introducing their manufacture, filling a demand created by the curbs in production elsewhere. After all, it provides both needed jobs and potential for economic development to benefit ordinary people. Unfortunately, some projections show that even if 90% of the countries currently producing CFCs were to cease production, a dangerous increase in atmospheric concentration of CFCs would be delayed but not prevented.

Second, it is not clear just what is happening to the ozone layer and why. It is difficult to get reliable data from the instruments used to measure it, and the results of some experiments have been faulted for untrustworthy instrumentation, the difficulty of calibration, for example. While most scientists are convinced that CFCs do in fact contribute to the depletion of the ozone layer, especially in the Antarctic, some are not convinced that this is happening elsewhere. To say that if CFCs increase, then the ozone layer will certainly be depleted is to go further than science in its present state can say. But there is considerable likelihood that that will happen, and those same scientists believe that steps to control production of CFCs are wise.

Technology tends to have effects that are quite unknown and perhaps unknowable, if not in theory at least in fact.

Case 3: Technology in Management

I take my third case, with some trepidation, from personal experience as the director of the editorial department of InterVarsity Press for sixteen years. I remember telling my own supervisor soon after my employment that I would never take the psychological profile test that was usually required for advancement in the organization. I did not—and do not today—trust those tests to give much useful insight. I believed—and still do—that they are unreliable at best and misleading at worst. Moreover, if after working with me for a few months my supervisor did not know all he needed to know about my qualifications for promotion, he was not likely to use well the results of a test.

Nonetheless, some fifteen years later in an environment in which I thought the results would not be misused or unduly twisted, I and other colleagues in my office did take such a test, one that was supposed to identify our basic temperament as we related to our tasks and relationships with others in the office environment. The test required us to match sets of words (I like words), and it took only five to ten minutes to fill out. We were all doing it together. The goal was to help us better understand ourselves and our relationships in order to increase our ease with each other and the efficiency of our work. What could be the harm?

Much, I am afraid. We all now know what style each of us turned out to be. Sophie, for example, is a high D. So am I. We both like to dominate. Frank is a high S; he is easygoing and likes stability. None of us learned anything we didn't already know about each other. Long ago my wife told me I have the "boss syndrome" (itself a term based on technology). But now we had scientific proof. And now there was every reason to harden our own self-identities and stereotypes of our colleagues. And we did.

The result of getting pigeonholed by others or of pigeonholing yourself is that it takes away the impetus to change, to grow, to learn to cope in wider situations. It is a detriment to improved relationships, because it is an excuse to keep them as they have been in the past. Once a high D, always a high D.

Do you see the technocratic mentality at work? Human contact, working side by side with our team, is not enough. So we use the techniques of psychological and sociological analysis to find out our coworkers' psychological profiles. No matter that many professional psychologists working with these techniques of analysis distrust their results.[11] We end up treating our friends as stereotypical psychological types, not as people. *Technique* alters and sometimes destroys human relations.

Even problems of church growth are attacked this way. We take a survey. We do an all-member canvas. We prepare a mailing to all the residents who are unchurched. We find out what people want in a church so that we can give it to them.

Now there is merit in *technique*. But there is also danger. The ubiquitous use of *technique* to solve all problems has taken from us our heart and soul.

Toward a Philosophy of Technology: Some Basic Principles

What, then, is technology? Look again at the definition of *technique* given above: "*Technique* is the *totality of methods rationally arrived at and having absolute efficiency* (for a given stage of development) in *every* field of human activity."[12] If this is technique, then *technology* is the whole field in which technique plays a decisive role. But isn't most of modern life permeated by technique? Indeed, yes, and that is why understanding its implications is so vital in developing a Christian mind. We will single out seven of them for special attention.

First, *technology as an embodiment of technique is value-laden.*[13] That is, technology is not dependent only on how it is used. It reflects the primary value of efficiency. And efficiency is measured in terms of time, energy and money. Among the methods available for accomplishing any given task we tend to choose a method which ranks high in at least one of those three categories. Mechanical tomato pickers rank high in all three.

But again, product or program technology does not ask what will be its personal impact on you, your friends or your society. The ready availability of an efficient solution to our problem adds technological pressure to social pressure. Whenever anything is readily available and attractive, there is always the temptation to use it. The lure of technology in an affluent society is hard to resist.

If as a reader you doubt this, I ask you simply to reflect on these questions: What have you wanted to buy in the past week? What have you wanted to do that is out of the ordinary this past month? What connection do each of these have with technology? What values are implicit in the decisions you have already made with regard to these desires?

Those are questions relating to individual, private values. What implications do our decisions have for the larger community? If you were an engineer designing a tomato harvester, what questions should you ask about (1) the character of the machine you were designing, (2) the potential impact its use will have on the total farming community, (3) the impact on the environment, (4) the impact on the consumer of tomatoes, (5) the impact on the economy?

The fact is that technology reflects human character. As the fellows of the Calvin Center for Christian Scholarship put it, "Technology proceeds out of whole human experience and is affected by the confessional, religious commitments unique to human beings."[14]

Second, *technology shapes society*. We saw this in the case of the tomato harvester. We will see it if the depletion of the ozone layer is in fact being caused by the increased presence of CFCs in our atmosphere. Technological objects do reshape society. If we do not pay attention to the probable implications of a piece of technology, we are simply doomed to having our society blindly molded by the material force of technology. Machines themselves will more and more come to dominate us, dictating what food we will eat, what clothes we will wear, how we will be housed, what games we will play, how we will express our love and wage our wars.

As Langdon Winner puts it, "Technologies are not merely aids to human activity, but also powerful forces acting to reshape that activity and its meaning."[15] Those of us like myself, who grew up on a small ranch surrounded by small family farms in the 1940s, have clear historical evidence of cultural change. Where are these small farms today? Vanishing rapidly. Why? Because it takes more and more land to support fewer and fewer families. Why? Because the farm equipment required to grow crops is today (1) much larger and more expensive, (2) capable of replacing many farm workers and (3) efficient only when it does so. So farms have become much larger and the farm population has fallen. Farm communities produce many more children than the community can support, and so they move to the cities.

What then has happened in the cities at the same time? Alan Jiggins summarizes it well:

> The drift to the suburbs has been a feature of life in Western society for the last fifty years. It is a logical development of a mass industrial and mass media society. The car, television, automatic washing machine, telephone and credit card seem to reduce the need for dependent social contact. We can now live unprecedentedly private lives with the aid of our socially isolating appliances.[16]

Technology has thus had a large shaping force on all our lives—rural and urban.

Third, *"technological objects . . . impose on the user the way in which they are to be used."* [17] Huge tractors cannot be used in small fields congenial to the terrain. The natural contours of land are thus disturbed to accommodate machinery. Erosion is the consequence. Computers require vision at a specific distance from the display. So users have to adjust the way they sit. New chairs are designed to accommodate them. Semi-trucks require expensive roads.

Thus emerges what Winner calls the "technological imperative" (the environment must be adapted to the machine) and "reverse adaption" (human ends are adjusted to match the technology).[18] If our machine can't do it for you, you can't have it. But you can and should have what our machine can do for you. In short, technological societies are a complex interweaving of technological objects with their support systems: TV, automobile transportation, food distribution. They require a vast network of other technological objects and the system to keep them going. These support structures are not neutral.

Fourth, *the effects of technology are not fully known.* This we saw in the case of the chlorofluorocarbons we are releasing into the atmosphere. Are they what is depleting the ozone layer? Will the radiation let in by this depletion be a serious threat to human health? We cannot, at least now, be sure. Even if we do our best to act responsibly on the knowledge we have, we may make serious mistakes.

One of the few discouraging words that engineer Samuel C. Florman has to say about technology is that its ill consequences do not result so much from deliberate human evil or even seemingly benign human error. "Even if engineering mistakes could have been eliminated entirely, the environmental crisis would have occurred just the same! The environmental crisis is upon us not for any single error, but because of an accumulation of apparently error-free decisions."[19] Nature, he says could respond to a few errors, even big ones like the construction of the Aswan Dam in Egypt or, we might add now, the oil spill off Alaska. But the accumulated decisions of many engineers, city planners, economists, business managers, politicians are too complex to control. People are too greedy. We will face crises as long as we are human.

Florman's response is to enjoy the "existential pleasures" that come from contemplating the beauty of the work of our hands. His solution echoes the once popular song "Don't worry! Be happy!" It is not one Christians can find appropriate. But his point should be well taken: solely as human beings we do not and cannot know enough to control technology.

Fifth, *technology changes the way we think about ourselves.* Long ago the ever-increasing complexity of computers gave rise to this question: Do computers think? Or, more poignantly, Are they persons? A similar question, for example, was posed on one episode of *Star Trek: The New Generation:* Does Data (an android who acts very much like a human being) have the "right" to decide whether he/it will be taken apart and analyzed on the hope of building an even better android? On the program, the answer was Yes. But this is science fiction. Well, maybe.

What is not science fiction is the effect the computer has had on how we think about ourselves. The computer, for instance, tends to shift our definition of who we are from Aristotle's *rational animal* (in which we distinguish ourselves from animals) to *feeling machines* (in which we distinguish ourselves from other machines, like computers).[20] Sherry Turkle has learned from her studies "that people who try to think of themselves as computers have trouble with the notion of the self."[21] Who are we? we ask in the computer age. The answer: "information processors."[22] What is really at stake, then, is not whether computers are persons, but whether persons are anything more than machines and, if so, what.

Sixth, *technology tends towards technicism—the religion of technology.* Technology's success in getting us to the moon, eradicating small pox, pacifying our physical desires and entertaining us endlessly entices us to see it as the final reality in our lives. It has become a god. Every time we have a problem we turn to it for a solution. The Calvin Center scholars say it well:

Technicism reduces all things to the technological; it sees technology as the solution to all human problems and needs. Technology is a savior, the means to make progress and gain mastery over modern secularized cultural desires. Technology thus becomes its own reason for existing.[23]

There is even a feeling of the sacred that comes from technology, says Ellul. And this is substantiated by Samuel C. Florman's ecstatic response to whirring dynamos.

The engineer's first instinctive feeling about the machine is likely to be a flush of pride. For all the mistakes that have been made in its use, the machine still stands as one of mankind's most notable achievements. Man is weak, and yet the machine is incredibly strong.[24]

After showing why engineers and scientists cannot be held responsible for the agonies caused by their products, Florman turns to poetry to express his own existential pleasure in contemplating the technical work of human hands. "Look long on an engine. It is sweet to the eyes," he quotes from poet McKnight Black."[25] And from a Mr. Ebeneser Elliott:

Engine of Watt! unrivall'd is thy sway.
Compared with thine, what is the tyrant's power?
His might destroys, while thine creates and saves.
Thy triumphs live and grow, like fruit and flower.[26]

If technicism is a religion, Florman is its liturgist. And General Electric with its television ad campaign that claims "We bring good things to life" is its evangelist.

The prophecy of technicism is simple: *If it can be done, it will be done.* And, of course, much can be done. There is *in vitro* fertilization of a woman's ova with a man's sperm—any man's. There follows research on "waste" zygotes (fertilized ova) that would otherwise have to be thrown away after a choice of zygotes had made the remainder "useless." There are massively expensive weapons systems that promise to keep pace with those of the "enemy." All possible. All inevitable. And all ethical. So says technicism.

For the ethics of technicism follows immediately: *If it can be done, it should be done.* In fact, doing it constitutes progress. And we mustn't get in the way of progress.

> Technicism says that humankind can use its hands and minds—its technology—to build a kingdom of plenty, ease and peace. Thus if something can be done, it should be done—no questions asked. "You can't stop progress."[27]

If our developing technology causes problems, dislocations in society, pollution of our environment, dysfunctional families, anxious people, no problem. Further, more advanced technology will solve these problems.

Seventh, *technology fosters a natural human urge toward the acquisition of power and control, the extension of the human sphere beyond its current bounds.* Bacon's "knowledge is power" has set the tone for the development of the modern world. Hans Jonas sums it up this way: "To become ever more masters of the world, to advance from power to power, even if only collectively and perhaps no longer by choice, can now be seen to be the chief vocation of mankind."[28]

This theme is central in *Star Trek* whose epigraph is "to boldly go where no man has gone before." Yet even this merely updates Mary Shelley's *Frankenstein*. There the narrator sets out on a journey to "satiate [his] ardent curiosity . . . and [to] tread a land never before imprinted by the foot of man."[29] Shelley's narrator goes on to indicate the price he is willing to pay for such an increase in knowledge and the power he thinks it will bring: "One man's life or death were but a small price to pay for the acquirement of the knowledge which I sought, for the dominion I should acquire and transmit over the elemental foes of our race."[30] Granted, it's his own life he has in mind. But it is but a small step from being willing to sacrifice one's own life to being willing to sacrifice the lives of others. This insatiable curiosity, reminiscent of Prometheus and Faust, always lurks in the shadows of the technological mind.

Responsible Technology: A Christian Approach

Technology poses tremendous problems for culture today. It has been with us, of course, since Adam was given the task of cultivating the garden. Noah could not have built the ark without it. But what makes technology so troublesome today is the availability and focus of massive power in small compass. With steam power came the industrial revolution; with electricity came the instant distribution of power all over; with the transistor came the miniaturization of data transfer. Now in our shirt pocket we can carry access to instant power.

But this newly acquired power has not been accompanied by a growth in social responsibility. We are no wiser in our use of a DC-10 jetliner than we were with the stagecoach of a century ago. Then we wore ruts in the prairie and shot all the buffalo. Today we pollute the atmosphere and send acid rain into our lakes. We write no better with a computer than we did with a quill. And we are likely to be no better at wielding the atomic bomb than we have been the hand grenade.

And there indeed is the rub. What does a Christian mind have to offer in response? In the matter of technology, how can we tell the difference between right and wrong? How do we get to know the good?

We cannot hope to answer such questions without knowing what the problem is. That has been the purpose of the preceding section. We have seen that a problem with technology is *technique,* a mindset that runs counter to the wholistic way in which we are made. It assumes values before it reflects on what they are. So *technique* must be subjected to severe criticism.

But being negative is not enough. Something positive is required. If we are not to live by technique, what are we to live by?

In one sense the answer is simple: "Seek first [God's] kingdom and his righteousness and all these things [food and clothing] will be given to you as well" (Mt 6:33). All we need to do is live by God's values. But what are they? That's when our task gets complicated, though not as complicated as we might think.

If we immerse ourselves in Scripture, especially if we examine the Gospels for "kingdom values" (the Sermon on the Mount from which the above quotation comes will make a good start), we will find lots to live up to. Primary, of course, is the positive virtue of seeking the good of others—first God's glory and then his reflected glory in other people made in his image. The two commandments summarizing the Ten Commandments put it in a nutshell: We are to love God with all of who we are, and we are to love others as ourselves. The Golden Rule is key here.

None of this is specific, however. We need to get a handle on just what role technology is to play in our lives and how we are to respond to its presence in our culture. Here is where my discovery of *Responsible Technology*, the result of work done at the Calvin Center for Christian Scholarship, became so valuable to me. What follows is largely based on the analysis of these six Calvin Center scholars: political scientist Stephen V. Monsma, communications professor Clifford Christians, economist Eugene R. Dykema, chemist Arie Leegwater, philosopher Egbert Schuurman and engineer Lambert J. Van Poolen.

First, it is necessary to reassess the definition of technology given at the outset, that is, technology as merely the application of *technique*. Since it loads the dice against seeing technology in any positive light at all, it is well to ask if there is not a way to see the products and tools we make as an aspect of God's creation. The Calvin Center scholars do just that. They believe the cultural mandate (which we discussed in chapter four) allows a positive role for technology. Adam and Eve were commanded not only to fill the earth but to "subdue" it (Gen 1:28). The word *subdue* does not justify exploitation but stewardship over the environment.[31] The job of the first human pair was indeed to "work it and take care of the [garden]" (Gen 2:15). This, the Calvin Center scholars argue, makes us "cultural agents" whose task, at least in part, is "to bring the creation into its full development."[32]

Seen in this light technology itself gets a new definition:

In essence we can define technology as a distinct human cultural activity in which human beings exercise freedom and responsibility to God by forming and transforming the natural creation, with the aid of tools and procedures, for practical ends or purposes.[33]

Notice that the concept of *technique* as defined by Ellul and operative in my original definition of technology has dropped out. Rational analysis may well go into the fashioning of tools and the mapping out of procedures, but it has disappeared as a ruling principle. Efficiency likewise disappears as a measuring rod of its success.

Still we are dealing in abstractions. More specifically how should technology be employed "to bring creation to its full development"? These scholars write:

Human beings are to subdue and rule God's creation, but in such a way that they bring out the beauty and excellence God has placed in his creation; they are to allow creation's potential to flower. In the process they become—paradoxically—ruling servants. They rule the creation in such a way that they also serve it.[34]

This they expand as follows:

Technology is to be done as a form of service to our fellow human beings and to the natural creation. This means we are to develop technology in such a way that the blessings, riches, and potentials God has put in creation are allowed to flower. We are called to do technology in such a way that the creativity and joy for which God created men and women can exist in abundance, the riches of the physical world can be uncovered and utilized, and the plant and animal worlds can be perceived and used for what they are and for what God intends them to be.[35]

Eight normative principles apply to technology, they argue. These are (1) cultural appropriateness, the fittingness of a product or procedure into the patterns of each culture; (2) openness of information about the procedures to all peoples involved; (3) stewardship of a bountiful creation; (4) the aesthetic norm of delightful harmony; (5) justice for all people affected; (6) loving care for them; (7) reliability or trustworthiness of the product or procedure; and (8) an attitude of trust toward God by whose care and bounty has come our technical ability.[36] The goal toward which the whole technological enterprise should strive is peace, *shalom*—resulting from the perfected relationships between God and humans, people with each other, and humanity with nature.[37]

General Electric may claim that they, with the vast diversity of their technological research, are bringing good things to life. But they are wrong. God alone does that. Without God even GE would not exist. But GE does exist and so do we. Surely many of GE's employees at every level are Christians. Is it not, then, part of our task—the task of GE's employees and customers—to help make "responsible technology" the heart and core of GE?

Bringing Good Things to Life

What can we learn about getting to know the good from the above attempt to take a Christian approach to technology? Perhaps it can be summarized in four general principles.

First, we need to know what the Scriptures say about how we should act toward one another and what kind of character we should be developing.

Second, we need to realize that our problems will not be solved solely by technique—whether it is a method of Bible study, prayer, worship or group dynamics, or a method of politics, science or technology. First comes not a method but an attitude—humility before God and silence before both God and others. Then comes prayer and worship and fellowship—the actions, not the method; the reality, not the theory.

Third, we need to understand the context of the issues we are concerned with. If we are to live a discipled life, we must probe deeply into the background. What is happening in medical technology must be known if one is to develop a Christian medical ethic or promote public legislation appropriate for our pluralist society. Not every Christian can do the tough work necessary in every area. But some Christians should be engaged in each. Every Christian should know a little bit about almost everything; some Christians should also know a lot about many things; others should strive to know all there is to know about a very few things.

Fourth, we need to know what Christians interested in the same issues are thinking. And we need to come into dialog with them at every level available to us—local Christian group, church, professional organization, international congress. It is good to be reminded that there are Christians like Dr. Linsley Gray, mentioned above, who work on the solution to problems of technology. We should seek them out in our own corner of the marketplace.

Fifth, we need to be humble searchers before we become teachers or activists. Because the implications of any technological device, program or process are rarely fully known, we are always in the position of making judgments on the basis of incomplete information. An open mind is necessary, though action is often required before we know all we would like to.

Sixth, as we do become activists, attempting to put into action the lifestyle and principles that emerge from our search, we need to respect all others as made in the image of God. No moral program, no spiritual principle, takes precedence over the dignity of any person—

believer or not, intellectual friend or enemy.

Getting to know the good in a pluralistic world is not easy. Doing the good is harder. But both are the logical implications of the discipleship of the mind.

But the intellect, which has been disciplined to the
perfection of its powers, which knows, and thinks while
it knows, which has learned to lessen the dense mass
of facts and events with the elastic force of reason,
such an intellect cannot be partial, cannot be exclusive,
cannot be impetuous, cannot be at a loss, cannot but
be patient, collected and majestically calm, because it
discerns the end in every beginning, the origin in
every end, the law in every interruption, the limit in
each delay; because it ever knows where it stands, and
how its path lies from one point to another.

John Henry Cardinal Newman[1]

Chapter 8
Getting to Know the World: The Academic Enterprise

All truth is God's truth. Science, in fact scholarship in general, functions because God is the Logos and the Logos made the world; it unlocks the meaning that God as the Logos (Meaning himself) put there. So scientists and other scholars, to the extent that they really understand the world, are thinking God's thoughts after him. This we saw in chapter five. Now we want to examine what it means in terms of the academic world and culture in general.[2] In this chapter we will deal with the natural and human sciences, in chapter nine with general culture, especially literature and television.[3]

All Truth Is God's Truth
One of the most troubling things we observe when we look at the results of much modern academic work, however, is that God is no-

where to be found. His existence is neither a part of the presuppositions on which modern scholarship is built nor the logical end of its implications. To a large measure, God's existence or nonexistence never comes into the picture. Laplace's dictum, "I have no need of that hypothesis," is systemic.

So, whatever a Christian might want to think to the contrary, most modern science proceeds on the assumption either that God does not exist or that his existence or nonexistence has no bearing on either the natural sciences and human sciences or the arts and humanities. Are then the results of academic study to be totally rejected by Christians? Is science done by Christians totally different from science done by non-Christians? No. Why? How can science proceed without regard to God and still come up with at least some truth about the universe?

The explanation lies in the nature of God, the nature of his created universe and the nature of human knowledge. All truth is God's truth, but not all claims to truth are true. We have seen something of who God and the universe are in chapter three and something of the nature of human knowledge in chapters five and six. Now we need to put these elements together in a new way to answer these further puzzling questions and to see how we as Christians are to relate to the academic world.

God has made the world as a uniformity of natural causes in an open system—that is, a system in which God himself may act.[4] The system is orderly because it exists as expression of a God who is Logos (reason, meaning). It is the existence of the universe as orderly and human beings as rational (a fuller expression of God as Logos) that sets up the foundation needed for science. If the universe always functions in the same way under the same conditions and if the human mind is capable of understanding, then experiments can be designed to demonstrate the accuracy of our human guesses (hypotheses) about the structure or working mechanisms of the universe. We can look and see, weigh and ponder, proceed by trial and error—all to the end that we come to grasp the underlying principles by which external reality (the physical world) works.

The concept of God is not a part of a strictly scientific explanation of nature. So long as we do not ask questions about the *purpose* of the universe (or any part of it), or about *why* it or anything else should exist at all, or about why we can *understand* our theories, the concept of God is not involved. Science only requires an implicit faith in the orderliness of the universe and our ability to understand it.[5] This faith is as present in naturalism as it is in Christian theism. Carl Sagan believes these things as much as Johannes Kepler. In other words, natural science done by naturalists and Christians is going to be similar if not identical.

Modern scientists who are naturalists, for example, do not object to Kepler's laws of motion though they might well reject his philosophy and religion or other extraneous ruminations not substantiated by evidence. Some of Kepler's attempts (for example, to explain the form of planetary motion) were indeed speculation based on preconceived notions of what perfect heavenly motion should be (circular) and how the size and shape of the orbits should relate to each other. As Charles Hummel says, "Kepler attempted to correlate the increasing distances of the planets from the sun with a combination of the five regular or 'perfect' solids of the Greek geometrists."[6] These speculations were not substantiated by the facts. So Kepler abandoned, though reluctantly, these ideas and stuck with what fit the observations open to public confirmation. It is on this that his reputation rests.

Christians may therefore expect to agree with the results of natural science, and they may participate as scientists with a good conscience, doing good scientific work.

It is when we move from the natural sciences of astronomy, physics and chemistry, however, and into the life sciences of biology (especially evolutionary theory) and the human sciences of sociology and psychology that conflicts between the so-called assured results of science and the views of Christians arise.

The most well known of all the conflicts comes from the field of biology. Since the publication of Darwin's *Origin of Species* in 1855, evolutionary theory has often been taken to challenge the biblical view of creation, especially the creation of human beings.[7] This conflict could well form the subject for the remainder of this chapter. But I have chosen not to discuss it for three reasons: (1) biology is well outside the range of my own expertise, (2) it is such a hot topic that those who disagree with my own view are likely to discard the general approach I want to commend toward all such problems and (3) the issue has been dealt with at length already by Christians of every persuasion—theologically, scientifically and philosophically, and I would have nothing of substance to add.[8]

I do, however, wish to discuss the conflict between the Christian faith and the social sciences. And I want especially to consider why these conflicts are so much more obvious and so much more intense than any found between the Christian faith and the natural sciences. Three reasons can be cited for this situation. The first and third are basic and systemic. The second is personal.

The Problem of the Human Sciences: Historical

The first reason involves history. Modern science began within the framework of Christian theism. Almost all the early modern astronomers were Christian in world view—Copernicus, Galileo, Kepler, Huygens, Newton.[9] The effect of their science was indeed to destroy the ancient Greek and medieval notion of the earth as the physical center of the universe and God as the Prime Mover of a system of circular (and thereby perfect) spheres. The motion of the planets was discovered to be elliptical and to be explained by the same physical laws as motion on earth. These new conceptions upset many Christians, challenging their world "picture," if not their world view. But the notion of an orderly universe did not undermine the notion of an orderly God; it was rather predicated on that notion.[10] Astronomers, in other words, assumed that the universe they were trying to understand was God's creation. The science of physics then developed parallel with astronomy; early physicists like Galileo were likewise Christians.

The human sciences, however, are a different matter. Auguste Comte (1798-1857), sometimes thought to be the first sociologist, was a naturalist. So were Sigmund Freud (1856-1939) and J. B. Watson (1858-1935), two early psychological theorists.[11] With the exception of C. G. Jung (1875-1961), whose basic world view is best described as pantheistic, all the early founders of psychology were self-confessed atheists. They were interested in religion but only as an expression of human desire, not as an expression of anything inherently divine in or beyond the cosmos. For them as much as for Carl Sagan, "the cosmos is all there is or ever was or ever will be."[12]

The subject of the human sciences is, of course, human nature. The goal is to understand human character and behavior. Since the assumption of these founders of the human sciences is that God does not exist, God can never be a part of any explanation or any theory. That situation, which is not so problematic in the natural sciences, becomes highly so in the human sciences. Why? Because, except for a few modern exceptions (far fewer than many think), all human beings are religious in some way. God, the gods, the divine, ultimate concern—these characterize us as people from the earliest times we know about to the conscious present. How can this be explained without invoking the existence of the divine?

Belief in God, for example, cannot be explained in the terms in which it is expressed by believers. They will understand it in terms of the actual existence of God. But many people doing psychology and sociology are naturalists who do not believe God exists. So they have to explain belief in God as an aspect of something else—our longing for a cosmic or transcendent Father (Freud) or the leftover memory of a primitive stage in our development (Comte) or the behavioral modification of our various societies still caught in the illusions of an earlier age (Watson).

If God does not exist, there is no way that human nature or behavior can have anything to do with God. This attitude pervades modern psychology and affects as well even the academic study of religion.

The Problem of the Human Sciences: Personal

There is a second explanation for the conflict between Christian faith and the social sciences, especially the academic discipline of psychology. It has to do with the kinds of religious convictions (or lack of them) that people drawn to psychology tend to have. Van Leeuwen remarks,

> There is evidence that, to this day, academic psychology in North America attracts persons who see in it a socially and intellectually acceptable way of evading, if not actually attacking, their Judeo-Christian heritage. A 1965 national survey of social scientists in university posts indicated that, even more than sociologists and political scientists, psychologists were indifferent or hostile to religion. Fully two-thirds of the psychologists interviewed said either that they were not at all religious or that religion was not a major force in their lives.[13]

And Van Leeuwen quotes some anecdotal evidence from psychologist Paul Vitz as well:

> The hostility of most psychologists to Christianity is very real. For years I was part of the sentiment; today it surrounds me. . . . In graduate school, religion was treated as a pathetic anachronism. Occasionally a person's religious beliefs were "measured" in personality tests. The common interpretation was that people holding traditional religious views were fascist-authoritarian types.[14]

Scientists, like everyone else, have prejudices that influence their behavior. Natural scientists, however, deal with nonpersonal matter—atoms, molecules, subatomic particles, stars, galaxies, rocks. An anti-Christian bias is not likely to affect the results of their work. Psychologists, however, deal with people, not just with their behavior, but with what their behavior means. Antireligious sentiment is bound to have a signal effect on their theories.

The Problem of the Human Sciences: Theological

The third reason for the conflict between the human sciences and Christian theism concerns the way in which the Fall has affected human knowledge. John Calvin provides the clue. In the Fall, says Calvin, "man's natural gifts were corrupted by sin, and his supernatural gifts withdrawn."[15] That is, our soundness of mind and ability to work in the world (our natural gifts) were marred and distorted; and our knowledge of God and the ability to act righteously (our supernatural gifts) were destroyed completely.

In other words, though all our ability to reason was affected by the Fall, our knowledge of God was affected far more than our knowledge of natural things. Our minds are still capable of functioning and giving us access to at least some truth. In fact, "to charge the intellect with perpetual blindness so as to leave it no intelligence of any description whatever, is repugnant not only to the Word of God but to common experience."[16] With regard to "heavenly things" (especially knowledge of God) "the most ingenious are blinder than moles."[17] With regard to "earthly things" ("matters of policy and economy, all mechanical arts and liberal studies") fallen human reason has not lost all its powers.[18] Fallen human beings can still be "acute and clearsighted in the investigation of inferior things."[19]

The point is this: the further the subject we are studying is from the character of God (that is, the less its essential nature reveals about God's essential nature), the more likely we are in our fallen unredeemed state to understand it. So those scientific explanations, theories and laws in fields like astronomy, physics and chemistry are less likely to be influenced by fallen human nature than are subjects like sociology or psychology; the latter have human beings for their subject matter, and human beings are made in the image of God. Studies in the humanities—literature, painting, the other various arts—have human culture as their subject matter, and they too will be more adversely affected than the natural sciences. Theology will be the most prone to error, for its subject is God, and our natural knowledge of God was the most to be affected. Here we are, as Calvin says, "blinder than moles."

So what are we to do as Christians trying to build a Christian world view? On the one hand, we should not dismiss all scholarship, all science, as so corrupt as to be totally wrong. On the other hand, we should not accept the so-called assured results of modern scholarship uncritically. Is there a way to discern? Is there a way to integrate what we learn through academic study with what we learn about God and his creation gained through Bible study and the work of the Holy Spirit in the redeemed lives of his followers? I think there is. Thinking worldviewishly about the academic disciplines is, if not all there is to it, at least a good place to start. So how does one do that?

Integration of Christian Faith and the Academic Disciplines

Thinking in terms of world views is a fruitful basis on which an integration of Christianity and academic study can proceed. In fact, world-view analysis provides, as well, a key to the evaluation of conflicting claims within the academic disciplines themselves. And thus world-view analysis can lead toward an integration of the academic disciplines among themselves.

We have already looked at what a world view is and at how world-view analysis proceeds. Two questions now remain: (1) how do world views function in relation to the academic disciplines? and (2) how does world-view analysis provide a basis for integrating our Christian faith and the academic disciplines?

World views have a symbiotic relation to the academic disciplines. On the one hand, every academic discipline is rooted in a world view. Or more pointedly, any given scholarly theory or perspective or way of studying the subject matter of any discipline is rooted in a specific world view. On the other hand, what one does in the laboratory or library affects the world view undergirding one's efforts. (See figure 7.)

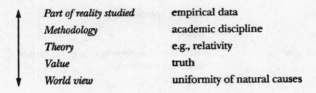

Part of reality studied	empirical data
Methodology	academic discipline
Theory	e.g., relativity
Value	truth
World view	uniformity of natural causes

Figure 7. World View and Scientific Study.

Looked at in one direction, the world view governs the values inherent in the science and places limits on the kind of theories that will qualify and on the methods that can be employed. It can even govern or limit the part of reality that is studied.

For example, if a scientist holds a naturalist world view, his or her values may well contain the concept of truth, but the resulting theories will have to be limited to nonsupernatural explanations. If a scientist holds a Christian world view on the basis of which all products of human conception are considered to be human, then certain methods will be avoided; the scientist, for example, will not experiment on human beings as did the Nazis nor use *in vitro* fertilization to produce material on which to conduct experiments as scientists today are tempted to do.[20]

But the thrust goes the other way as well. Often scientists do not reflect on the world view undergirding their scientific endeavors. They simply "do science." That is, as members of a community of practicing scientists they merely go about their business. But that business itself—the methods that have become standard in the field—determines the kind of theories that will result. Behaviorists, for example, rule out any data of human self-perception and deal only with external behavior. The possibility of learning anything about dreams or intuitions is eliminated from the outset. (See figure 8.)

Part of reality studied	human behavior
Methodology	measuring of stimulus/response/reinforcement
Theory	operant conditioning
Value	truth
World view	naturalism (uniformity of natural causes in a closed system)

Figure 8. Behaviorism and Its World View.

Freudian methods, on the other hand, thrive on the data of dreams. Human nature, including the interior of our mental processes, is part of the reality studied. The theories resulting from this are quite different than those resulting from behaviorism. (See Figure 9.)

Part of reality studied	human nature
Methodology	dream analysis, myth analysis
Theory	id, ego, super ego
Value	truth
World view	naturalism (uniformity of natural causes in a closed system)

Figure 9. Freudian Psychotherapy and Its World View.

Let us look in more detail at how world views relate to one theoretical construct in modern psychology.

Behaviorism and the Christian Faith

The field of psychology is rich in alternate theories and approaches, having taken many divergent branches in its development over the past hundred or so years. There is no end to the strains we might look at. And it is a pleasure to say that Christian psychologists have been doing just that, especially in the past fifteen years. Mary Stewart Van Leeuwen has been publishing in this area for much of this time, examining, for example, such approaches as cognitive psychology and studies in AI (artificial intelligence).[21] Her own proposal for a Christian personality theory illustrates the sort of work that can be done and should be done much more extensively by Christian social scientists.[22]

But theories in these areas have become highly complex in recent years and are often difficult for people not trained in the field to understand. Fortunately there is at least some major aspects of one branch of psychology—behaviorism—that are fairly accessible to nonspecialists. Moreover, while major tenets of behaviorism are rejected by many psychologists, it is still having an impact on the way education courses are taught in many colleges. Most important for our purposes, however, is that the extreme form in which it has been expressed by its major proponent, B. F. Skinner, allows us to see how tension can develop between Christianity and an academic discipline.

B. F. Skinner has been working for decades to develop a "technology of behavior."[23] The center of the system he has developed—a system called behaviorism—is the concept of "operant conditioning." This he first propounded over fifty years ago in 1938.[24]

Skinner demonstrated that

a three-term formulation is necessary to describe how an animal or human being is induced to change its behavior. . . . The three necessary terms are stimulus, behavior, and reinforcement. Their relation can be symbolized as follows:

$$S^B R \ldots S^B R \ldots S^B R \ldots$$

The lower line represents the environment's action on the organism and the upper line represents the organism's actions on the environment. S is the preliminary stimulus situation; B is some behavior the organism may then show or "emit"; and R is then any change or "reinforcement" from the environment which is *immediate* and *contingent* on a particular B.[25]

Let's take an example and say that S is a Good Humor man. B is to buy and eat an ice cream cone. R is a pleasurable sensation. This R will serve to reinforce B when S is again present.

I like this illustration because it reverses a childhood experience in which S was a soda counter in a drugstore, B was eating an ice cream cone, and R was heaving in a ditch on the way home. I didn't eat store-bought ice cream for several years.

If Skinner were only describing such homey situations as this, or if he were to limit the applicability to the kind of operant conditioning we use to break horses, house-train pets and so forth, no one would have much objection. His work would fit into the Christian world view as easily as a naturalistic one. But Skinner maintains that all human behavior is to be explained by such chains of stimulus-behavior-reinforcement so that any notion of a person's acting out of an autonomous "character" of his or her own is totally discounted. "A person does not act on the world, the world acts on him," writes Skinner.[26]

If we read Skinner's *Beyond Freedom and Dignity* worldviewishly, we can learn the presuppositions that underlie his behaviorism and see that it is not the concept of operant conditioning itself that is the problem but the framework in which he sees it fitting. Let us ask, then, a few basic world-view questions of Skinner:

1. What does Skinner see as the really real? Apparently the universe itself is self-existent. Skinner, though born and raised in a Christian home, has rejected any concept of God and is a confirmed naturalist.[27] The universe is a uniformity of cause and effect in a closed system. There is nothing transcendent. Thus there is no God who could act

on his creation according to his own will and perhaps foul up the perfect lock-tight determinism required if operant conditioning is to explain all behavior.

2. What is a human being? Here Skinner is clear, "Man is a machine in the sense that he is a complex system behaving in lawful ways, but the complexity is extraordinary."[28] These lawful ways in which we behave as human beings presuppose a complete determinism: "Personal exemption from a complete determinism" Skinner writes, "is revoked as scientific analysis progresses, particularly in accounting for the behavior of the individual."[29]

Moreover, there is no "self," no inner man, possessing demon, homunculus: The self is rather, "a repertoire of behavior appropriate to a given set of contingencies."[30] So, if you change the environment, you change the *self*—which isn't really a self anyway, but just a bundle of potential behavior.

3. What happens to a person at death? Here Skinner is ruthlessly consistent. Death is extinction of the personality. "When I die," says Skinner's alter ego in his novel *Walden Two,* "I shall cease to exist— in every sense of the word."[31]

We could go on to discuss Skinner's notion of value, his suggestions for changing our society into a utopia and so forth. But what I have said here is enough to show the direction in which world-view analysis can proceed.

I do wish to point out, however, that it is not enough just to unmask and observe Skinner's world view; we should also go further and point out the implications of holding such a view—its tendency toward elitism, its promotion of manipulation as a social good, and so forth. And we should note, too, its inner inconsistencies. For Skinner's view on its own terms cannot be known to be true. Despite its claim to be objectively true, the theory itself undercuts the possibility of truth. Let's see how that is so.

If all human behavior is completely determined, so is Skinner's behavior. Therefore, Skinner had to write what he wrote. We had to read it (or not) and accept it (or not) on the basis of our environment and what we were conditioned to be before we came to his book. You too had to read this book. I had to write it. You had to agree with me or not. None of us—out of ourselves—decided anything.

Therefore, if Skinner's view is true, what it says is either (1) trivial for it could not make any difference to how we decide or (2) only a mechanical link in the chain of causality which brings about the future.

In any case, none of us—including Skinner—could check the truth or falsity of the theory, for all our logical mental operations would be subject to the same restrictions as Skinner's theory itself. So if the view is true, no one could *know* it to be true; that is, there would be no justification for anyone's belief that it was true. To know something is true, there must be an "autonomous" person; part of a person (the self) must stand beyond the system of cause and effect and be able to *see* by a standard not wholly within the frame. A transcendent self is necessary if we are to avoid *epistemological nihilism.* Christianity provides for such a transcendent self; Skinnerian behaviorism does not.[32]

To sum up, then, all academic disciplines and their attendant theories (many of which conflict) are grounded in often unexamined presuppositions—conceptions often taken to be so true that no alternative has ever occurred even to some of the profoundest scholars. It is these world views which we need to identify, analyze and critique if we are to integrate our faith and our academic study.

We need also to look at the other side. What we do in the laboratory affects our theorizing, our values and even our world view. If we never study the spirituality of human beings, we will never make any theories about it or challenge the naturalism on which almost all modern psychology is built. And as Christians, if we simply adopt the methodologies of psychology, we will never be able to counter the destructive impact of psychology on our self-understanding. We will tend to come to adopt the notion that the most important things we can know about ourselves is what can be taught us by using the methodologies of academic psychology. What then will happen to the key notion of who we are as human beings—the image of God?

A Basis for Integration

So, we ask secondly, how does world-view analysis provide a basis for integrating our Christian faith and our academic disciplines? The answer takes several forms.

First, world-view analysis allows us to *discover* and *examine* the underlying presuppositions of every academic theory and every discipline. As we have seen, it is not behaviorism's observations about behavior per se that conflict with our faith but the presuppositions undergirding the understanding of the observed behavior that lead to false conclusions. By examining the total framework of any academic insight, we can discern at least partially where potential strengths and weaknesses lie, where we might go wrong if we were to incorporate its conclusions into our Christian world view.

It is, for example, not appropriate to conclude that Skinner's behaviorism is the psychological complement to Christian theology's doctrine of the binding, enslaving power of sin.[33] The two notions are inherently incompatible, for one assumes individual human integrity and responsibility before God. It sees human beings in their Godward dimension. Skinner's concept of a human being as reactor only, a being without a responsible ego-center, a "complex repertoire of behavior," requires that there be no God for this being to be in relation to.

As Bruce Nicholls puts it,

The secular anthropologist and sociologist [and, I would add, psychologist] approach the study of culture [and human nature] from a different perspective. They assume that the world is a closed system and that all factors of cultural [and personal] formation, including the religious one, are contained within the system and determined by it, so that claims to knowledge of supra-cultural realms [or transcendent selves] are themselves the product of the systems.[34]

If God is really there, however, and not just a product of our fertile imagination looking for a ground of being, then Skinner's psychology is at heart in error. And while there may be many insights that can and should be integrated into our Christian understanding of behavior, we need not as Christians feel ourselves being pulled away from our fundamental understanding of reality.

Second, world-view analysis allows Christian to identify the biblical presuppositions that can undergird proper scholarship. If we know from Scripture, from revelation, that human beings have a Godward dimension that affects their human behavior in a crucial way (and this we do know), we will not be essentially Skinnerian in our study of behavior. We may, of course, find a place for "operant conditioning" as a "useful model" to explain some behavior or to allow us to shape other human behavior. But its exaltation to an explanation of all human behavior will not do.

The Scriptures present people—even after the Fall—as responsible human agents who do not simply salivate when a bell rings. They themselves act from the inside out—to be sure with input from the outside in—and thus are creatures with an ego, a central personal core.

In other words, we have in world-view analysis the possibility of promoting a specifically Christian approach at least to the social sciences.[35]

Newman's Vision

Third and finally, world-view analysis provides a basis for interdisciplinary studies. I am convinced that the real questions we need to ask and answer about God, human beings and the universe are not going to be answered exhaustively by any one academic discipline. As John Henry Cardinal Newman writes in *The Idea of a University*, "All branches of knowledge are connected together, because the subject-matter of knowledge is intimately united in itself, as being the acts and the work of the Creator."[36] Knowledge is a whole—a unity. Each "bit" relates to other bits and is only known for itself when it is seen in its proper place as a *part* of the larger *whole*.

No matter what *appears* to the contrary, if we could see with the eyes of God, we would perceive the oneness of all truth—the truth of biology and the truth of Genesis 1, the truth of Freud (if any) and the truth of B. F. Skinner (if any). What each has perceived that is truly the case would be found to be in harmony.

As Newman put it, "Hence it is that the Sciences, into which our knowledge may be said to be cast, have multiplied bearings on one another, and on internal sympathy, and admit, or rather demand, comparison and adjustment. They complete, correct and balance each other."[37]

It is on this basis that Newman erects the goal of education:

That only is true enlargement of mind which is the power of viewing many things at once as one whole, of referring them severally to their true place in the universal system, of understanding their respective values, and determining their mutual dependence.[38]

Or again:

But the intellect, which has been disciplined to the perfection of its powers, which knows, and thinks while it knows, which has learned to lessen the dense mass of facts and events with the elastic force of reason, such an intellect cannot be partial, cannot be exclusive, cannot be impetuous, cannot be at a loss, cannot but be patient, collected and majestically calm, because it discerns the end in every beginning, the origin in every end, the law in every interruption, the limit in each delay; because it ever knows where it stands, and how its path lies from one point to another.[39]

Or again:

> That perfection of the Intellect, which is the result of Education,
> and its *beau ideal*, to be imputed to individuals in their respective
> measures, is the clear, calm, accurate vision and comprehension of
> all things, as far as the finite mind can embrace them, each in its
> place, and with its own characteristics upon it. It is almost prophetic
> from its knowledge of history; it has almost supernatural charity
> from its freedom from littleness and prejudice; it has almost the
> repose of faith, because nothing can startle it; it has almost the
> beauty and harmony of heavenly contemplation, so intimate is it
> with the eternal order of things and the music of spheres.[40]

Viewed from the end of the twentieth century these visions of the
educated person seem like rhapsodic dreams. I know of nothing like
this in today's literature of education. Newman's vision of unity and
his optimism regarding the capacity of the human intellect is, I think,
as foreign to today's typical university mindset as it is to Christians
facing that mindset. Newman here sees no tension at all—neither
between his faith and reason, Christianity and scholarship, nor between one academic discipline and another. There is one truth in
general, and each elucidation of parts of it—each academic discipline—fits together neatly.

Does the academy today embody Newman's vision? Hardly! We are,
largely, a despairing people—that is, we despair of visions of unity.
Our world is in fragments. There is nothing central or firm that
anything relates to. Everything is relative; nothing is absolute. Things
do not cohere. Skinner will not sleep well with Freud. Albert Camus's
world is essentially incompatible with the world of Saul Bellow. Milton
Friedman's economics is hardly that of E. F. Schumacher. The insight
of Gerard Manley Hopkins that "the world is charged with the gran-
deur of God" is countered by Stephen Crane's declaration that the
universe couldn't care less about us.

Indeed, Newman's vision is not realizable this side of glory. But it is predicated on an ideal. The theory is right. God is there to be both the cause and end of our thought. Truth is one. It is just that in our fallen state with the proliferation of world views and with the foundation of much academic work on the premise that God does not exist, we are not likely to realize Newman's hope. But the ideal still stands, like Jesus' notion of the kingdom of God, as a goal worth striving for.

World-view analysis will set us on the way. What is a human being? is addressed by literature, linguistics, history, philosophy, physics, chemistry, biology, physiology, psychology, sociology, theology and so forth. Each provides a glimpse. And it is questions like Who am I? How can we live together? What shall we do about violent crimes and the violent criminal? that are the important issues of life. World-view analysis in all of our academic disciplines will help get the most significant questions to the surface.

I began reading books, reading books to delirium. I began by vanishing from the known world into the passive abyss of reading, but soon found myself engaged with surprising vigor because the things in the books, or even the things surrounding the books, roused me from my stupor. . . . Books swept me away, one after the other, this way and that; I made endless vows according to their lights, for I believed them.

Annie Dillard[1]

Chapter 9
Getting to Know
the World:
The Cultural Enterprise

*I*f "the heavens declare the glory of God" because God created the heavens, then culture, too, declares the glory of God because God's creatures created culture. Unfortunately, culture also declares the corruption, error and ignorance of its human creator. So the study of culture produces a mixed bag of insights into the way things really are. For some of the things we learn through human culture are true and some quite false.

Jesus walked through the streets and byways of Palestine affirming some aspects of its culture and tipping others on their heads. As he was the best guide to culture then, through his Word in Scripture he is our best guide now. Richard Niebuhr in *Christ and Culture* outlines five ways Christians have understood Christ's relation to culture: (1) opposition, Christ opposed to culture; (2) agreement, Christ is what

162 ◀ DISCIPLESHIP OF THE MIND

culture says he is; (3) synthesis, Christ and culture are both of value with Christ forming the center; (4) dualist (paradoxical), Christ and culture pull in opposite directions, but both have to be dealt with this side of glory; (5) conversionist, Christ is the transformer of culture. It is simplistic, but nonetheless helpful, to say that fundamentalists usually are found in camp (1), liberal Christians in camp (2), Catholics in camp (3), Lutherans and neo-orthodox Christians in camp (4) and Calvinists in camp (5).[2]

The first two of these positions are, I believe, seriously flawed. The first assumes that a community can exist with Christ so at the center that it is well-nigh perfect. This view actually leads to the establishment of enclaves of Christians, subcultures that have their own fallen character, separate communities like the Amish who have little to do with anyone but themselves. The second position interprets Christ by the standards of culture. That has meant in the West that Jesus must not have performed miracles because miracles are not possible.

The other three views are more biblical. Without arguing for it, however, let me simply state that the notion undergirding this book and this chapter is the last one: Christ transforming culture. It is, I believe, our task as Christians to understand the values Jesus espoused and Paul explained, and then to help transform culture by the expression of these values in the world around us. But that is getting ahead a bit. We will develop this notion in the final chapter.

In this chapter, I simply want to investigate further ways to understand culture. We will look first at literature, an aspect of high culture. Then we will examine television—on the other end of the cultural scale—looking at the role it plays in both reflecting and shaping cultural values. Along the way, we will glance at newspapers and other popular print media.

Reading the Literature of the World

Literature—like the arts in general—forms a major window on human culture. Through the great works of poets, novelists and essayists we see the multiple splendors of the world. Great art is not the province of one world view only. It is found in every major one. Art sets its world view in bold relief against its contenders in the marketplace. In literature life is writ larger than life.

Therein lies a major value for Christians. Getting to know good literature is getting to know human beings as they are seen to be from a wide range of perspectives. We learn, in other words, what all sorts of people think makes all sorts of people tick.

But because literature embodies various world views, it should be read with the mind awake. The key to reading well, I believe, is to read worldviewishly. Essentially this involves reading with the seven worldview questions (see chapter two) in the immediate backdrop of our consciousness, asking them of each piece we read. Doing this helps us grasp not only the particular thoughts and attitudes displayed on the surface of the text but helps us see as well where the author is coming from and why he or she is saying what is being said. It helps us place the author and text in a larger cultural context.

The main benefit of reading the best sort of literature, however, is not just to know what someone else is saying and thus pick up information or perspective. It is not even to reinforce one's own particular Christian understanding of God or his creation. The main benefit, rather, is to help us understand who we are as a human family in all our diverse and glorious yet fallen splendor.

The best literature makes us feel what it would be like to hold other views of the world. It helps us get inside mindsets very different from our own. That is the reason I have prefaced each chapter of this book with one or more well-written quotations. Each text was chosen, not only because it says what I want to say, but because it embodies that thought in eloquent language—language that conveys more than appears on the surface, that sets up sympathetic vibrations in us as readers, that both focuses our mind on the ideas and sensitizes us to the personal dynamic of those ideas.

What is it like to hold the views of a Zen Buddhist? There is no better way to find out than to learn to read the haiku poetry of the great Japanese poet, Matsuo Basho (1644-94). Why do modern Jewish people look back so much on the horrors of the holocaust? Read Elie Weisel's *Night*. What does it mean to be an existentialist? Read Jean-Paul Sartre's *Nausea* or Albert Camus's *The Plague*. What fueled the imagination of the beat generation and made its principal characters tick? Read Jack Kerouac's *On the Road* or the poetry of Allen Ginsberg or Gary Snyder.

Where have we come from? What did we use to think and feel? The sweep of world literature from the earliest times of the Greeks and Romans in the West and their counterparts in India, China and Japan, to the latest poem or novel—these are the best texts to provide the world's various answers to the third world-view question: *What is a human being?*

It is the literary character of the Hebrew Scriptures, the Old Testament, that most helps us reconstruct the mindset of the ancient Hebrews. The Psalms not only provide texts for worship, but reveal the shape and feel of biblical faith in ways not possible in the more straightforward prose of the Law, for example. The prophets call us in ringing poetry to return to principles set down in the Law. The parables are powerful in large part because they are superb literary structures. And the Gospels likewise do their work in our minds and hearts because of their unique literary form.

The Task of Literature

Joseph Conrad once described the task of the literary artist this way:

> To arrest, for the space of a breath, the hands busy about the work of the earth, and compel men entranced by the sight of distant goals to glance for a moment at the surrounding vision of form and color, of sunshine and shadows; to make them pause for a look.

for a sigh, for a smile—such is the aim [of the serious writer], difficult and evanescent, and reserved only for a few to achieve. But sometimes, by the deserving and the fortunate, even that task is accomplished. And when it is accomplished—behold!—all the truth of life is there: a moment of vision, a sigh, a smile—and the return to an eternal rest.[3]

Literature, in other words, embodies a *view of reality* (reflecting the world view of the writer) that is captured in *concrete terms (rather than philosophic terms) and given a linguistic structure* which is appropriate to the various ideas and attitudes that make up the view of reality and which will evoke an *appropriate experience* of these ideas and attitudes in a *skilled reader*. What better way to understand another's view of reality than to experience it vicariously through great literature?

Since I have already written an entire book *(How to Read Slowly)* on all kinds of literature—popular and sophisticated, poetry, fiction and prose—I will limit my discussion to only a few examples drawn from poetry.[4] That will serve to illustrate how reading literature of all types can disciple the mind. Each of the poems I have chosen deals with nature. And each represents one of the three main world views we have been contrasting throughout this book—Christian theism, naturalism and pantheism.

What gives each poem its special appeal, however, is not the general views it conveys but the specific experience of specific versions of these general views. There are many Christian poets and many poems embodying Christian ideas. But there is only one Gerard Manley Hopkins. In fact, among the many poets I admire, Christian or otherwise, Hopkins is clearly my favorite.

Hopkins: Dappled Skies
British poet-priest Gerard Manley Hopkins (1844-89) was in his own eyes first a priest and only with reluctance a poet. He destroyed his early work when he entered the Jesuit order and left unpublished all

his subsequent poems. We will look at one, "Pied Beauty," a very modern poem, nonetheless echoing the Hebrew psalms.

I want to warn anyone who is not already a reader of poetry that most poems do not yield their full effect, or maybe even their plain-sense meaning on a first reading. Poetry expresses what cannot be expressed in any other way, and it usually does so by compression. Few words make much sense. But that means that these words will have to be read with great care. The following poem and most others by Hopkins will be worth every minute—even every hour—spent with it.

Pied Beauty

Glory be to God for dappled things—
    For skies of couple-colour as a brinded cow;
      For rose-moles all in stipple upon trout that swim;
Fresh-firecoal chestnut-falls; finches' wings;
    Landscape plotted and pieced—fold, fallow, and plough;
      And all trades, their gear and tackle and trim.
All things counter, original, spare, strange;
    Whatever is fickle, freckled (who knows how?)
      With swift, slow; sweet, sour; adazzle, dim;
He fathers-forth whose beauty is past change:
                         Praise him.[5]

The verbal texture in this poem is rich, and on first reading the thrust of the poem may not be clear. But with a few slow, attentive readings, the poem yields its basic meaning and begins to work its magic on our mind and heart.

Like all great poetry, "Pied Beauty" should be read over and over, often aloud, until its rhythms sink in and its shape takes form in our own mind. That can't be done in a book but only by a person. I can only urge readers to take the time to do this even before reading the following explanation.

The first task in reading this poem is, of course, to be sure we know the meaning of all the words. Poets, always conscious that they should say things exactly right, often stretch our vocabularies and send us to a dictionary. Here are definitions of some of the more peculiar words in this poem:

pied: spotted, mottled (like the pied piper)

dappled: spotted or variegated in color

brinded: irregularly streaked

stipple: painting with tiny dots

fallow: land left unseeded after plowing

Some of the unfamiliar words are combinations of familiar ones and can easily be figured out. For example:

rose-moles: mole-sized spots the color of roses

Only one may require knowledge not readily available.

fresh-firecoal chestnut-falls: red-hot chestnuts that have fallen through the grate on which they are roasting

With these definitions in mind, the poem becomes accessible and can be paraphrased quite easily:

Praise God for many-colored things—variously colored skies, spotted trout, roasted chestnuts, bird's wings, farm land, tools of various crafts—every thing that's multiple. God creates the rich assortment of our environment. Praise him.

In short, Hopkins is simply praising God (who is the changeless One) for making the world (which is many and changing all the time).[6] The title says it even more succinctly, "Pied Beauty."

But the paraphrase is *not* the poem. It is just a guide to get us into the text. It is the poem itself—its rhymes and rhythms, its imagery and syntax, its structured build-up and climax—that triggers our response as readers.

Here indeed is a poem which captures the feel of a theistic view of nature. The multiple-colored profusion of the world is a glorious expression of God in his ingenious creativity—if the viewer but be there to see it. Most of us would miss it. Gerard Manley Hopkins does not. And word-crafter that he is, he presents his vision to us via a paean of praise to God the Father-Creator.

Hopkins can teach us who are not poets to look closer at nature, see it through the eyes of faith and give glory to God the Father. Hopkins also praises Christ in his poetry. In "The Windhover," for example, he compares Christ to dying embers that when they "fall, gall themselves, and gash gold-vermilion." In this image of Christ's spilt blood as both red and gold, Hopkins juxtaposes the gory and the glorious, and captures the adverse beauty of the cross: the crucifixion, the slaying of the Son of God, is one of the most violent acts in human history and the fullest expression of God's love. Throughout his poetry Hopkins's Christian world view comes through at every point.

Hardy: The Thrush and Hope beyond Despair

At the turn of the twentieth century, British poet Thomas Hardy (1840-1928) likewise saw in a nature a backdrop to his own emotion, but for him an emotion of growing despair. Born and raised a Christian, Hardy abandoned his faith early in life, but he could never replace the emotional stability it offered. One of his most well-known poems, "The Darkling Thrush," captures for us the tenor of naturalism. If God is not there, is there any hope for anyone?

The Darkling Thrush

I leant upon a coppice gate
 When frost was specter-grey,
And Winter's dregs made desolate
 The weakening eye of day.
The tangled bine-stems scored the sky

    Like strings of broken lyres,
And all mankind that haunted nigh
    Had sought their household fires.

The land's sharp features seemed to be
    The Century's corpse outleant,
His crypt the cloudy canopy,
    The wind his death-lament.
The ancient pulse of germ and birth
    Was shrunken hard and dry,
And every spirit upon earth
    Seemed fevourless as I.

At once a voice arose among
    The bleak twigs overhead
In a full-hearted evensong
    Of joy illimited;
An aged thrush, frail, gaunt, and small,
    In blast-beruffled plume,
Had chosen thus to fling his soul
    Upon the growing gloom.

So little cause for carolings
    Of such ecstatic sound
Was written on terrestrial things
    Afar or nigh around,
That I think there trembled through
    His happy good-night air
Some blessed Hope, whereof he knew
    And I was unaware.[7]

This poem is somewhat easier to understand than Hopkins's "Pied

Beauty." There are a few unusual words, but the syntax is straightforward, considerably more so than most poems by Hopkins.

darkling, in the dark
coppice gate, gate in a wall of thickets
Century's corpse, the end of the nineteenth century
crypt, burial vault
illimited, unlimited

"The Darkling Thrush" forms an interesting contrast to "Pied Beauty"! Both see in nature a reflection of deeper meaning. Both see
birds—one concentrating on the variegated color of a finch's wing,
the other on a bird beruffled by the blast of wintry wind. Hopkins's
poem is set in the clear light of day, Hardy's at dusk. Hopkins sees
beauty in diversity; Hardy can only hope that the frail, gaunt, maybe
even dying bird knows something about the coming century he does
not. For Hopkins there is the glorious fecundity of God, his rich
fathering-forth. For Hardy there is only the death throws of a century
which brought loss of faith to him and all of Europe. For Hopkins the
heavens declare the glory of God; for Hardy there is no God and thus
no glory. There is only the beautiful but mournful call of a "darkling"
(no "fresh-firecoal" here) thrush casting with its last breath its soul
into the dying world.

Basho: A Frog and an Ancient Pond

Our third example comes from Japanese haiku poet Matsuo Basho
(1644-95).

On a bare branch
A crow is perched—
Autumn evening.[8]

This poem is, of course, a translation from the Japanese language, but
it retains much of its poetic quality, though not its seventeen syllables
which is the Japanese haiku form. It is the epitome of simplicity—
merely one image which catches the tone of autumn, arresting, as

Joseph Conrad would say, "for the space of a breath" the motion around us. But there is no interpretation, no stated mental "meaning"; the bare (thus autumn) branch and crow do not stand for anything. They are merely a branch and a crow, seemingly set in silhouette against the autumn sky.

How can this embody a world view? Good question—with a good answer. But to get to it let's look at another Basho haiku.

An ancient pond
A frog jumps in—
The sound of water.[9]

This poem, too, is short, deceptively simple, fundamentally profound. Read from a solely Western, let's say American background, this haiku is as minimal as poetry ever gets. It directs the attention to one context (an ancient pond), one moving object (a frog), one result (the sound of water being entered by a frog). But this is enough—enough to take our minds off the hurly-burly of ordinary life—country or city. In Conrad's words it "compels" us "to glance for a moment at the surrounding vision of form and color, of sunshine and shadows; to make [us] pause for a look, for a sigh, for a smile."

As Christians reading this poem and understanding it in theistic terms, we might feel that there is more going on than this. The poem reminds us of the objectivity of God's created order. There it is!—the stable substructure of the universe (the ancient pond), the moving finger of time (the jumping frog), the intersection between the two setting up the possibility of consciousness—the ability of people created in God's image to catch the flow of time in its flight, at least long enough to make the created order consciously present to us—certainly a blessing of God. But Basho was a Zen Buddhist, not a Christian. His intent, whatever it was, could not have been to have his poem read as a modern Christian might read it.

Looked at with some understanding of its actual cultural context in Zen Buddhism, the poem takes on a very different cast. One goal of

Zen literature is to tease us out of thought, to so focus our attention on the here and now—or as in this poem on the intersection between the eternal and the temporal—that we lose our minds and realize our unity with the really real. In Zen Buddhism that really real turns out to be the Void, the Nothingness from which all temporal forms come.[10] In Zen there is no God to create the universe; there is only the sound of water—the almost temporal intersecting with the eternal. In arresting us from the workaday world Basho's poem both expresses his Zen grasp of reality and sparks in us a vicarious feeling of what being a Zen Buddhist is like.

Seen in the light of the second haiku, the first one quoted begins to take on meaning: This is all there is to autumn—two utterly silent elements. This is all there really is to the world—its simple thereness, a form without further meaning. Let me quote without comment two other haikus by Basho. How is the Zen grasp on reality present?

The sea darkens,
The cries of the sea gulls
Are faintly white.[11]

A cuckoo—
Far out where it disappears,
A lone island.[12]

Literature in the Academy

The approach I have taken to literature in this chapter is quite traditional. It has not taken into account much modern literary criticism, especially the schools of reader-response criticism, structuralism, post-structuralism or deconstructionism. At the moment these approaches, which focus on language rather than human experience, are not widely used in undergraduate courses in literature. More and more, however, they are affecting the classrooms, and certainly graduate students will have to learn to deal with them.

Describing the confusing scene in literary criticism today, Leland Ryken writes:

> Underlying many of the critical schools today . . . is a prevailing nihilism. Its commonest form is skepticism about the ability of language and literature to communicate precise meaning. The most extreme form of this nihilism is, of course, deconstruction. This influential movement is rooted in theories that view language as an arbitrary system of signs. Adherents of this theory typically reduce a text to a series of contradictions and ambiguities in an attempt to show that it has no discernible meaning.[13]

He goes on to describe how one teacher dismantles W. B. Yeats's "Sailing to Byzantium" into "an endless web of contradictions" so that by the end of the class students learn that, in the words of the teacher, the "true 'meaning' of 'Sailing to Byzantium' . . . is the impossibility of ever arriving at a true meaning."[14]

Moreover, while the discipline of literary study has been "alarmingly secular for a long time," Ryken notes that it is "increasing in hostility to Christianity." Jonathan Culler, one of modern criticism major figures, charges that literary criticism, as it has been practiced, is far too Christian. "He claims that teachers of literature have 'abandoned the historic mission of education,' which is to 'fight superstition and religious dogmatism,' " and he bemoans the fact that he voted to fund a scholarly session on the Hebrew Bible, a text he now calls "powerfully racist and sexist."[15]

These schools of literary criticism may well be rapidly passing fads or "fashionable absurdities" (as Robert Alter calls them). Or they may leave a lasting mark on the teaching of literature in college or high school. That remains to be seen.[16] For a consideration of the proper response of Christian literary scholars to these movements, I will merely refer readers to Leland Ryken's essay and a response by Clarence Walhout. See also the literature section of the bibliography at the end of this book.[17]

Keeping Up with the Joneses: Television and the Newspapers

Literature and the other arts are the sophisticated end of culture—as Matthew Arnold would say, "the best that has been thought and said in the world."[18] Television is the main exponent of the popular end of culture—one might say the "worst that is currently being thought and said in the world." And yet it engages and bids fair to shape us all, especially in America, in ways that, if we really reflected on it, we would find repulsive. "Television," writes media critic Neil Postman in an excellent analysis of television's impact on society, "is our culture's principal mode of knowing about itself."[19] If we want to keep up with the Joneses, that is, understand what the Joneses are thinking and doing, television cannot be ignored.

Television, then, like literature is a window on our world. Everything about it tells us something about ourselves and our culture. The network news doesn't tell us much that will help us understand what is really going on. For that we will need to listen to the *MacNeil-Lehrer Report*. But network news will tell us what information and perspective people are getting from which they make their decisions and live their daily lives.

Some specials and documentaries on public television are accurate and penetrating in their analysis. And occasionally a network drama or comedy series will display keen insight into the human condition or make shrewd social commentary. A short-running series called *Max Headroom*, for example, was a brilliant satirical critique of the very medium of which it was a part—television. But as Neil Postman says, "Television is at its most trivial and, therefore, most dangerous when its aspirations are high, when it presents itself as a carrier of important cultural conversations."[20] As I write this, America is in the midst of a presidential election campaign. Virtually nothing significant can be learned either from the images portrayed by television or the sentences crafted by the candidate's speech writers for use on television. I have been listening carefully for several months for either major candidate to state clearly what any of his foreign policy will be. How will either one approach the current trouble spots of the world? Silence.

The problem is that images cannot handle sustained thought. Only words can do that. "Whenever language is the principle medium of communication—especially language controlled by the rigors of print—an idea, a fact, a claim is the inevitable result. The idea may be banal, the fact irrelevant, the claim false, but there is no escape from meaning when language is the instrument guiding one's thought."[21] Yet more and more newspapers, led by *USA Today,* are using the techniques of television—filling their pages with super-short stories without context and therefore without significance. There are only a handful of newspapers worth reading in the United States, and they should mostly be scanned for items of genuine value. There is no general significance to the fact that a young child fell down a well in Texas, nor is the story of her rescue of anything but sentimental value. Nothing whatsoever hangs on such stories—except the circulation of newspapers and ratings of television.

On the other hand, says Postman, "The best things on television *are* its junk"—when television does not aspire to teach but to entertain.[22] And television entertainment expresses in vivid form the social values that permeate our society. Television sitcoms, for example, both reflect and promote social mores. Some, like *All in the Family,* have tried in fact to be pacesetters. Others, like *The Bill Cosby Show,* seem to promote traditional values. And still others—the bulk of them, I think—are like *The Love Boat;* they just ride the wave of decadence.

What, then, is life like on the sitcoms: Happiness is associated with money, sex and power. The best cars, house, clothes, entertainment are the most expensive. Individualism—"I did it my way"—is promoted without concern for the public good or even the good of one's more immediate family. Fathers are weak and bumbling; children are morally wise. Broken homes are okay—just something to be dealt with. Cops or detectives with pseudo-Eastern, nonrational intuition solve crimes. People are depicted in morally compromised situations as if they were the norm. In one sitcom, a young girl lives with two men, either of whom could be her father and both of whom she treats as her father, pleased that she doesn't know which one it is. There is nothing wrong in sex outside of marriage, just be sure it doesn't hurt anyone around you. The popularity of such moral drivel is a graphic index to America's mores.

Postman is therefore wrong to say that such programs as *The A-Team* and *Cheers* are "no threat to public health" if he means moral health. When decadent morality is portrayed as normal, this morality seeps into the consciousness of viewers who at their best moments know better. Their sense of decency is thus unwittingly eroded. Their best moments become fewer and fewer, till they may disappear completely. If you are older than thirty, consider how your own attitude to the sinfulness of sex outside of marriage has changed over the past fifteen years.

Notice, finally, what television does to religion—in particular, Christianity. Either (1) the programs are straightforward broadcasts of church services, in which case they lack the very essence of corporate worship—its corporate quality—or (2) the programs become sheer entertainment. In the first instance the Christian faith is shorn of *koinonia,* fellowship, our connection to one another in the social order. We become lonely consumers of someone else's singing, a foreign community's prayers. Of course, such programs do remain a real help to people who are confined to their homes. But they are no substitute for the real thing. In the second instance the very message of the Christian faith is distorted out of all recognition. Idolatry—the substitution of the fake for the genuine—is the result.

Postman puts it bluntly but fairly:

You shall wait a very long time indeed if you wish to hear an electronic preacher refer to the difficulties a rich man will have in gaining access to heaven. The executive director of the National Religious Broadcasters Association [an evangelical organization] sums up what he calls the unwritten law of all television preachers: "You can get your share of the audience only by offering people something they want."

You will note, I am sure, that this is an unusual religious credo. There is no great religious leader—from the Buddha to Moses to Jesus to Mohammed to Luther—who offered people what they want. Only what they need. But television is not well suited to offering people what they need. It is "user friendly." It is too easy to turn off. It is at its most alluring when it speaks the language of dynamic visual imagery. It does not accommodate complex language or stringent demands. As a consequence, what is preached on television is not anything like the Sermon on the Mount. Religious programs are filled with good cheer. They celebrate affluence. Their featured players become celebrities. Though their messages are trivial, the shows have high ratings, or rather, *because* their messages are trivial, the shows have high ratings.

I believe I am not mistaken in saying that Christianity is a demanding and serious religion. When it is delivered as easy and amusing, it is another kind of religion altogether.[23]

Christians shouldn't have to hear this from a secular critic. We should have known it all along. But not only do many of us not know it, we deny it by our actions every time we broadcast trash. Developing a Christian mind surely means hearing and doing the truth when it is so obvious.

Better Wells, Better Water

If television and the newspapers are such poor sources for solid information and analysis of the important issues of life, where can we go? How can we develop the kind of discernment we need for life in a complex world. I suggest selecting one weekly news magazine, like *Time* or *Newsweek*, one periodical book review, like *The New York Times Book Review* or *The New York Review of Books*, and one magazine of cultural commentary, like *Atlantic Monthly* or *Harper's Magazine*. Add to this periodicals that specialize in your particular area of interest. All of these are better than the newspapers or television. But they too need to be read with discretion—that is, with a Christian mindset. Looking beneath the surface of a news story and how it is told, asking world-view questions about its form and content, investigating the background of the essayist, will often reveal bias and distortion.

Christian publications like *Christianity Today* or *The Reformed Journal* should also be a staple in your diet. Of course, there is no final contemporary authority on our society—no book in the library, no periodical that gives us *the* Christian view. We will always have to pay attention to all forms of information and analysis, and then make up our own minds, realizing all the while that our views are only partial and maybe downright wrong.

A Community Project

Inevitably it is easier to describe the sorts of things an individual might do to keep abreast of culture than it is to figure out what our Christian communities can do. But we must remember that we are communal creatures; we should do at least some of this keeping up together, reading and discussing key social issues with our friends. Scheduling special times with our Christian friends to hash out both important immediate issues (for example, whom to vote for) and long-range concerns (for example, how as Christians we should become involved in politics locally and beyond).

Some groups of Christians meet regularly to discuss a significant book—like *Amusing Ourselves to Death*—selected by a member who has read the book or has been reading book reviews and can select wisely. In our church the adult education program often includes a class on culturally significant issues.

We are all immersed in culture—pop and sophisticated. We need each other's help in figuring it all out. The discipleship of mind is indeed a community project.

The Christian claim that the whole and only meaning of history before and after Christ rests on the historical appearance of Jesus Christ is a claim so strange, stupendous, and radical that it could not and cannot but contradict and upset the normal historical consciousness of ancient and modern times.

Karl Löwith[1]

Human destiny [is] an episode between two oblivions.

Ernest Nagel[2]

Chapter 10
What's It All About?
The Meaning of
Human History

*T*he story of humankind—what's it all about? Does it have a meaning? Is God in charge, shaping events to conform to his ultimate if inscrutable will? Or is human destiny, in Ernest Nagel's words, just "an episode between two oblivions"?[3] Or maybe everything that happens will happen again, as imagined by the Hindus with their notion that all history is cyclical. Nietzsche found solace in just such a notion:

> Nietzsche, having decided that God is dead, knew with vertigo that he danced on the edge of the abyss; and not until he felt he could embrace the most senseless and repulsive possibility—Eternal Recurrence of the same meaningless sequence—did he feel safe ground under his feet.[4]

Or maybe we are about to enter a New Age of peace, heralded in the

skies by the Harmonic Convergence touted by New Age aficionados
in August of 1987.

Where, if anywhere, is history going? Expressed as the seventh
world-view question, this is the issue we will look at in this final
chapter.

Question 7: What is the meaning of human history?

The Context of the Question

In our happy moments when life seems to be going our way, we lay
aside many tough questions. We seem oblivious to the frustrations of
our own life and the tragedies in the lives of others. But just let
someone prick the bubble protecting us from our memories and we
are barraged with questions that we find too painful to think about,
let alone answer. And that is because any answers these questions may
have seem distant and often unconvincing.

We may be reminded that the life of a college student in our own
community has been snuffed out in an automobile accident, a man
in the prime of life has died of cancer, a child has been born grossly
deformed, a mother has become an alcoholic and left her children,
a husband has beaten his wife senseless, a pastor has died of AIDS,
a young man's brains have been fried by drugs. Teenage gangs run
the streets of the inner city; drugs are sold on street corners, men
father children and leave them to their mothers and the state to care
for; mothers have abortions or stuff their unwanted children in trash
cans or raise them to enter society maimed by malnutrition and lack
of parental care; landlords oversee slums and rake away profits. These
are our communities.

Beyond the city, the suburbs and farms, nations battle nations
openly and covertly. America supplies arms to Iran and Iraq. Iran and
Iraq use them against each other. Terrorists take hostages and assas-
sinate statesmen and bystanders alike. The mass murders of Hitler
and Stalin are replicated in South East Asia as Pol Pot and the Khmer

Rouge execute millions of Cambodians. This is the world.

A century ago, in Charles Baudelaire's poem "Travelers," a world-weary traveler reports that "chief among all the wonders of what we glimpsed in every corner" was "the boring pageant of immortal sin."[5]

It has always been like this—wars and rumors of wars, personal tragedies and national catastrophes. It is not hard to stimulate a deep sense of sadness and despair by thinking along these lines. Our usual method of maintaining a bright spirit involves ignoring, suppressing or deliberately avoiding knowing about such matters. A better way is to think about them within the framework of a Christian world view, contemplate them till we gain some sense of satisfaction that there is a meaningful scheme in which these seeming absurdities fit.

The Raging of the Nations

The issue of whether history means anything or not is an old one. In Psalm 2 one psalmist, for example, handled the problem this way:

Why do the nations conspire
  and the peoples plot in vain?
The kings of the earth take their stand
  and the rulers gather together
against the LORD
  and against the Anointed One.

And he went on to answer his question by seeing the situation as God sees it.

The One enthroned in heaven laughs;
  the Lord scoffs at them.
Then he rebukes them in his anger
  and terrifies them in his wrath, saying,
"I have installed my King
  on Zion, my holy hill."

In this coronation psalm, celebrating the installation of a new king in Israel, the psalmist sees all the violence the surrounding nations would wreak on Israel as totally in the control of God.

But there is much more. The psalmist sees that the king that is being installed has a special relation to God, and he quotes the already installed king as proclaiming a decree from God.

I will proclaim the decree of the LORD:
He said to me, "You are my Son;
today I have become your Father.
Ask of me,
and I will make the nations your inheritance,
the ends of the earth your possession.
You will rule them with an iron scepter;
you will dash them to pieces like pottery."

A king with this status—having been made a son of God—will take charge. He is to be feared by all the lesser nations surrounding Israel. And so the psalmist warns and advises them:

Serve the LORD with fear
and rejoice with trembling.
Kiss the Son, lest he be angry
and you be destroyed in your way,
for his wrath can flare up in a moment.
Blessed are all who take refuge in him.

This psalm well befits a coronation ceremony. But immediate historical reality was somewhat less than this vision. Israel and her kings did not fare well in subsequent history. David's kingdom was first divided, then the Northern Kingdom fell to Assyria and a couple of hundred years later the Southern Kingdom and Jerusalem itself fell, sacked by the Babylonians and utterly destroyed. God's people were taken into exile, and it was some seventy years before any came back to rebuild the temple and the walls of the city. It looked like the psalmist's vision failed.

By Jesus' time Psalm 2 had begun to be associated with the coming Messiah and in fact is "one of the most frequently quoted and alluded to" in the New Testament.[6] Jesus' teaching about the kingdom of God (Mk 1:14-15) made the connection apt and implicit. When the address of God to the king in the psalm, "You are my Son," became God's address to Jesus at his baptism (Mt 3:17) and his Transfiguration (Mt 17:5), the connection became explicit. Moreover, the apostle Peter, speaking before the Sanhedrin, quoted the opening two verses and associated Herod, Pilate and the Gentiles with the "kings of the earth" and Jesus with the "Anointed One" (Acts 4:25-27).

But Jesus as the Anointed One did even less to bring his enemies to bay than the earlier kings of Israel. He established no reign; he rejected violence as a lifestyle. In fact he let them execute him. As Paul writes to the Philippians, Jesus "did not consider equality with God something to be grasped, but . . . became obedient to death—even death on a cross!" (Phil 2:6, 8). It was through death that victory came. But that has removed the king from his kingdom!

Neither Jesus nor the Davidic kings ever exercised worldwide dominion, and history since Jesus is still replete with wars and rumors of wars. The fact is, therefore, that either the Bible is wrong about the ultimate triumph of God and his people or something is yet to come. And that is indeed how Psalm 2 is interpreted by the final book of the Bible. Text after text reflects its imagery. "The Revelation, in the symbolic and mysterious language of its writer, contains an anticipation of the ultimate rule and triumph of the man born to be King in the language and imagery of Ps 2 (Rev 1:5; 2:27;4:2; 6:17; 12:5; 19:5 and others)."[7]

The Already and the Not Yet

Meanwhile we are in interim period. In fact all of history, as seen by the Bible is interim between beginning and end. The beginning is in a garden where humankind began in harmony with God. The end is in a city lit solely by the glory of God where God's people again will live in peace. The middle is the muddle that began with the Fall and the expulsion from the Garden and ends only when the Lord returns in triumph over sin and death, puts an end to the wars and rumors of wars, and makes way for the New Jerusalem, four-square and radiant, to descend from heaven.

Karl Löwith puts it clearly: "Man's sin and God's saving purpose— they alone require and justify history as such, and historical time. Without original sin and final redemption the historical interim would be unnecessary and unintelligible."[8] In short, history is linear, a meaningful sequence of events leading to the fulfillment of God's purposes for humanity.[9]

God has given us a period between the Fall and the final redemption in which we see played out his yearning to bring his fallen people back to himself. We see his call to Abraham to make a single people for his name, his selection of Moses as the leader to bring his people out of bondage in Egypt, his selection of David the king who was to symbolize his sovereignty over the nation of Israel and all other nations, his selection of Mary to be the mother of the God-man Jesus. And then we see Jesus as the Christ—the Messiah, the Anointed One of Psalm 2—announce the coming of the kingdom of God, teach his disciples the way of the kingdom, then become himself the sacrifice for the sins of all humanity from Adam through the last ages of earth. We see him rise from the dead as the first fruits of the resurrection, showing his own triumph over evil, demonstrating his deity, and guaranteeing that his followers too may look forward to a resurrected life with God and all his people in the age to come.

So as the Israelites before Jesus looked forward to the coming of the Messiah, we look forward to the coming of the king who will wrap up history and lead us into an eternity of abundant life. Already God has shown us that while we were yet sinners, Christ died for us. Already he has shown us what a life lived for God looks like. Already he has called us to follow him in a life that may well lead as did his to suffering and death. Already he has shown us in his resurrection that we are valuable to God as individuals far down into the reaches of eternity.

But not yet do we see the rulers of the world brought under his reign. Not yet do we see all tears wiped from our eyes. Not yet do we see removed the corruption of the human spirit expressed in culture. We still see disease and sickness, the anguish of losing sons and daughters to drugs, rape, violence and war.

This interim period is the age of the *already and the not yet.* So we look in hope toward a future that we as yet see only dimly and solely by the light of the Scripture. Human history is not, therefore, a tale told by an idiot signifying nothing. It is rather the unfolding story of God's creation, our rebellion, his redemption and our future glory with him.

In Medias Res

So here we are *in medias res,* in the middle of things, in the middle of history. There is no going back, no returning to a time before the Fall. We are children of Adam and Eve. Moreover, we did not call ourselves into being. We arrived on the scene and only gradually have awakened to where we are. We are a bit like ten-year-olds as Annie Dillard describes them.

Children ten years old wake up and find themselves here, discover themselves to have been here all along; is this sad? They wake like sleepwalkers, in full stride; they wake like people brought back from cardiac arrest or from drowning; *in medias res,* surrounded by familiar people and objects, equipped with a hundred skills. They know the neighborhood, they can read and write English, they are old hands at the commonplace mysteries, and yet they feel themselves to have just stepped off the boat, just converged with their bodies, just flown down from a trance, to lodge in an eerily familiar life already well under way.[10]

When we begin to build a Christian world view, we find ourselves in precisely the same place. We are already here. We already have a world view. Oops! What is it? Is it anything like what is really the case? And so begins the journey which, if we remain awake, does not end till Jesus takes us to be with him and we no longer "see through a glass darkly" but see him "face to face" and unafraid find all our questions answered (1 Cor 13:12, AV).

But we are not there yet—face to face with our Savior. We are here in a fallen world in which the kingdom of God has been inaugurated but not brought into fruition. How shall we then live? What should we do?

The Presence of the Kingdom

We have looked at some answers to those questions in chapters six through eight. Now I want to give a final perspective on the questions and suggest a direction, not just for us as individuals, but for us as the church, for us as communities of believers. Lesslie Newbigin, it seems to me, has put the challenge better than anyone else:

> The church is the bearer to all the nations of a gospel that announces the kingdom, the reign, and the sovereignty of God. It calls men and women to repent of their false loyalty to other powers, to become believers in the one true sovereignty, and so to become corporately a sign, instrument, and foretaste of the sovereignty of the one true and living God over all nature, all nations, and all human lives. It is not meant to call men and women out of the world into a safe religious enclave but to call them out in order to send them back as agents of God's kingship.[11]

What are we to do? We are to bear the gospel to *all nations.* That is, we are to be global in our mission: Christians in all nations bearing the gospel to people in all other nations. The gospel is not the property of Christians in America or England or any Western or Eastern nation—a property to dispense to the rest of the world. Transnational, crosscultural evangelization is a task for Christians in every country in the world. In short, from all nations, to all nations.

The *gospel* is not a stripped-down message of personal sin and salvation. It *announces the kingdom, the reign and the sovereignty of God over all nature, all nations and all human lives.* Jesus Christ is Lord over all. His kingdom values should permeate our political, social, educational, entertainment and business networks and systems.

The cultural mandate has not been revoked. We are still to be stewards of the created order; we are still to be "making culture" by our actions within society. We are to be "salt and light" to the world we live in. And it is at least the suggestion of the Scripture, if not its very clear teaching, that some of what we do as human beings will be preserved in the celestial city. After John, the writer of Revelation, sees the New Jerusalem coming down from above, he sees the kings of the earth bringing their splendor into the city (Rev 21:22). The good in human culture is being lifted up to glory.

The Sermon on the Mount is not an ethic only for a future utopia, a millennial reign. Its principles should be embodied not only in our lives at church and among believers but should become the unwritten law inscribed on our hearts and the backdrop to the consciousness of even those who do not believe. This is our task within culture— to live by, encourage others to live by, and if necessary for us to die by.

The sin we are called to repent includes our *false loyalty* to other powers—the cultural powers (individualism, materialism, careerism, professionalism) that overtake us, the fall to the temptations common to all (pride, greed, envy, lust, sloth, anger, gluttony). As we grow as Christians, we will become more and more sensitive to sin, more aware that what looked like a minor peccadillo is the tip of a submerged iceberg of unconfessed and unrecognized moral depravity. Repentance means sorrow, confession and a turning around toward a new life honoring to God who calls us to be perfect even as he is perfect (Mt 5:48).

Then the church as a body is to become first a *sign* of God's sovereignty, an indication to the world that our God reigns in our lives. The church is to show what God's rule is really like, not to show how good and wonderful the church is, but to point beyond itself to the one it serves. It should become a sacrament, an outward expression of the inward presence of Christ, in the corporate body. "Surely," Jesus said as he departed from his disciples for the last time, "I am with you always, to the very end of the age" (Mt 28:20 NIV).

Second, the church is to become an *instrument* of God's sovereignty, claiming the rule of God over all creation. We are to act, not just wait for God to do things without us. As our minds are being discipled, we are to disciple other minds. "All authority in heaven and on earth has been given to me. Therefore go and make disciples of all nations, baptizing them in the name of the Father and of the Son and of the Holy Spirit, and teaching them to obey everything I have commanded you" (Mt 28:18-20).

Third, the church is to become a *foretaste* of God's sovereignty. Our communities should be characterized by kingdom values. When people on the outside look in on us, when they visit our gatherings, when they see us living and working together, when they observe the work we do in the world outside our own groups, they should be drawn by the sweet savor of the aroma of Christ himself.

We are not called out of the world into safe Christian *enclaves* where we exist only in and for ourselves. We are called together to prepare for going out, for leaving the stability of known relationships, the safety of situations we know we can handle, the ease of tasks we have done before. We are to take up the tough jobs of living out kingdom values where kingdom values are ridiculed—where taking time with God, instead of partying at night and sleeping in in the morning, is thought to be madness, where taking the right job for the kingdom is taking the lowest-paying job on the market, where taking five years to get a B.A. in English or six to get a B.S. in engineering gets you stares of disbelief, where living near the poverty level when you could be on your way to a penthouse loses you your place in the societal sun, where entering a medical field puts you in danger of losing your life to AIDS, where choosing to live a lifestyle that challenges the values of your neighborhood so that your own children begin to wonder what's wrong with you, where raising your children to honor the sovereignty of God makes life tough for them too.

"My kingdom is not of this world" (Jn 18:36), Jesus said, not to distance himself from the workaday world of his day, but to proclaim that life under God's reign is strikingly different from the life of a Pilate or a Sanhedrin bent on preserving their place in the social pecking order.

The Cross and the Meaning of History

In a striking final chapter of *The Politics of Jesus,* John Howard Yoder says, "Christians in our age are obsessed with the meaning and direction of history. Social ethical concern is moved by a deep desire to make things move in the right direction."[12] As a result, he continues, we look for "handles" we can grasp to move things in the direction we think they should go, aspiring to jobs of influence in education, business, advertising, even religious organizations. The assumptions are (1) that the direction of history can be managed, (2) that we know enough to manage it and (3) that the effectiveness of our efforts is itself a "moral yardstick."[13] But these assumptions are more than dubious not just in light of our miserable failures to control events when we try but also in light of the moral yardstick of Jesus' own life.

Yoder believes we should look at the cross of Jesus as the key to human history—not just as the center point of history where God redeems his people from their sins but as the key to what history is all about.[14] And as we noted above, Jesus chose to reject the temptation to rule as governor or king. He let himself fall under the machinations of evil men. We are to expect no less as we glorify God by imitating Jesus and living out kingdom values.

The imitation of Christ is for Yoder an important facet of being a Christian, but, he argues, it has in Scripture only one focus.

Only at one point, only on one subject—but then consistently, universally—is Jesus our example: in his cross. . . . The believer's cross must be like his Lord's, the price of his social nonconformity. . . .

"The servant is not greater than his master. If they persecuted me they will persecute you." (John 15:20)

is not a pastoral counsel to help with the ambiguities of life; it is a normative statement about the relation of our social obedience to the messianity of Jesus.[15]

What does history mean, then, for a disciple of Christ? It means that Christ and his church are engaged in embodying the values of the kingdom of God in such a way that suffering will become a way of life. Suffering is, of course, already a way of life for all people, some more, some less. But suffering which is not brought on or endured for the sake of Jesus and his kingdom is absurd. Nonbelievers sense this and rail against God, "Why me! Why my family!" And they sink deeper into despair as they fail to acknowledge that most suffering has been brought on by the Fall and by the sins of the fallen, that God is indeed sovereign over all, that God in Christ has himself suffered for the sins of the world and taken on himself the blame for all of us.

Philippians 2 "affirms a philosophy of history in which renunciation and suffering are meaningful," the only view of history that is worthy of belief.[16]

The Discipleship of the Mind

We have come a long way in our journey from the beginning of wisdom to the end of history. The task of developing a Christian mind has been seen to be long and arduous, but exciting as well. There is beauty and truth and goodness and joy in setting our hand to the plow and, though the soil be hard and the day be long, not looking back.

As our lives pour forth in obedience that takes us into suffering, let us be like coals in a dying fire that "fall, gall themselves and gash gold-vermillion."

Moses was educated in all the wisdom of the Egyptians and was powerful in speech and action.

Stephen to the Sanhedrin[1]

Then the king [Nebuchadnezzar] ordered Ashpenaz, chief of his court officials, to bring in some of the Israelites from the royal family and the nobility—young men without any physical defect, handsome, showing aptitude for every kind of learning, well informed, quick to understand, and qualified to serve in the king's palace. He was to teach them the language and literature of the Babylonians. . . . Among them were some from Judah: Daniel, Hananiah, Mishael and Azariah.

Daniel[2]

Appendix
Thinking Your Way through College: For Christian Students in a Secular University

I n this book I have dealt with issues that are relevant to any thinking Christian out of the university or in—faculty or student. I want now to discuss ways students can think Christianly as they do their academic work. If you are a student, I would like to address you directly. Think of me as a kindly professorial uncle (fathers have little authority these days).

If you want to make your time in college worthwhile—an experience of genuine education in which you are deliberately trying to think God's thoughts after him—give these suggestions some thought. Then put into practice the ones that apply most to you.

Get an Education
1. To be educated is to have at least a passing acquaintance with a

broad range of ideas. So take as many general humanities courses as you can squeeze into your academic program. Or take an extra year at it. If you are planning to be an engineer, or a doctor, or an accountant, enroll in art history, surveys of English or world literature, music appreciation, philosophy. If you are majoring in the humanities, take a few science courses even if they are not required. I especially recommend literature courses for social science majors, for I believe that at least as much can be learned about who we are as human beings from literature as from the social sciences.

2. Take advantage of the fact that books of all types are available to you regardless of your chosen specialty. Annie Dillard once asked her Chinese interpreter about getting a book from a public library in China:

"What if you were an engineer and wanted to borrow a book of literature?"

To my astonishment Song Hua burst into laughter. He doubled over as if kicked, he gasped for breath, he hugged his ribs and stamped his foot. I looked down the back of his neck. Gradually his head rose again; his face was splintered with hilarity. He gave me a sidelong "oh, you card" look, and said, as clearly as he could, "But you couldn't . . . if you were an engineer . . . get to read . . . a book of literature!" And off he rolled again into squalls of laughter.[3]

3. Take the tough courses in everything. Avoid the ones you can sleep through.

4. Choose courses that match. If you are a history major, when you study eighteenth-century Europe, enroll in eighteenth-century English literature. And vice versa. You can write papers that will both integrate your learning and dazzle your professors.

5. Take courses in "the philosophy of" your subject; find out what intellectual presuppositions undergird your profession. Courses like literary criticism, the philosophy of science, the philosophy of educa-

tion examine the foundations of thought in these respective disciplines. They are often not required in an undergraduate program. But take them as an upper-class student anyway. They will raise the questions you should be asking of your studies, even if the answers examined are not Christian.

Roll with the Punches

6. Don't be afraid of unusual ideas that challenge your own views. And don't be afraid of challenges to Christianity. So what if your professor finds out you are a Christian and thinks you must be a "fascist-authoritarian type"? You know better. The intellectual underpinning of the Christian faith is as strong if not stronger than that of the alternatives. You may not understand this as you first face individual challenges, but you will as you scramble for answers.

7. Speak up in class. Ask questions that make both you and your professor think. Intellectual sparring will help rid you of bad thinking and will strengthen your mental muscles. You will have more of a mind with which to worship God.

Seek Community

8. Find others in your classes who are Christians. Get together with them to share your academic concerns in the context of Christian community. In your InterVarsity chapter or college Christian fellowship, form subgroups to (1) discuss the challenges you face in the classroom, (2) deal with the implications of your studies for your Christian faith and your Christian faith for your discipline, (3) pray specifically for each other, your professors and classmates.

9. Sponsor lectures by local and visiting faculty and professionals on the relationship between their discipline or profession and the Christian faith. Listen to those who have been wrestling with these issues and have the wisdom that comes from experience.

10. If your university has a Christian study center nearby, like the

Center for Christian Study near the University of Virginia or the Mac-
Kenzie Center near the University of Oregon, take some courses in
religion, theology or Bible. Often, too, Christian professors from your
secular university will offer at the center special courses integrating
Christian faith and their academic discipline. These can be priceless.

11. Whether or not your course work takes a Christian perspective
into account, develop on your own a solid understanding of the Christian world view. This book is just a start. Move on to books like Brian
Walsh and Richard Middleton, *The Transforming Vision;* Charles Malik, *A Christian Critique of the University;* David Gill, *The Opening of the
Christian Mind;* Harry Blamires, *The Christian Mind* and *Recovering the
Christian Mind;* and Gene Edward Veith, Jr., *Loving God with All Your
Mind.* See the bibliography at the end of this book for details of
publication and further suggestions.

Study Worldviewishly

12. Ask world-view questions of your textbooks and your professor.
For example, in psychology, ask: What does Skinner (or Freud, or
Maslow or Piaget) think it means to be human? What distinguishes
people from other forms of life? What are our basic problems as
human beings? How can they be solved? Compare the answers you
get to the way you respond as a Christian.

13. Read books and articles by Christian professionals in the fields
you are studying. Thirty years ago when I was an undergraduate, few
Christians were doing serious academic work as Christians. Today
there are hosts of Christians in most academic fields, some at the very
top of their professions. Find out who these are in your areas of
specialization. Read their work. Attend professional meetings and
meet them personally. They will be delighted to encourage you and
at least send you away with arms sagging from a heavy bibliography.
See the suggestions in the bibliography of this book for places to start.

14. Join the professional organization of Christians in your academ-

ic field and attend their local or national meetings. The American Scientific Affiliation, for example, has been serving Christians in both natural and human sciences for some forty years. Its journal alone, *Perspectives on Science and Christian Faith* (formerly the *Journal of the American Scientific Affiliation*), is worth the dues of the organization, which are reduced for students anyway. Other organizations are listed in the bibliography of this book.

15. Write papers integrating your understanding as a Christian with what you are learning in your courses. Don't write to evangelize your professors, but to express your growing understanding of how your faith relates to your academic work.

16. When professors seem especially helpful, talk with them after class. Meet with them in their office or over a cup of coffee in the union. Find out how the things they teach and think are lived out in their own lives. You may develop a rapport that will allow you to let them know your goals and aspirations as a Christian.

17. If you find yourself getting in over your head, seek Christian friends and share your questions with them and your pastor or Inter-Varsity staff worker. Lots of Christians have sunk before they swam. But when they finally surfaced, they have swum longer and further than those who just let professors ferry them across the academic waters.

Don't Worry about Grades

18. Don't worry about grades. Be in college for an education. Grades might help you get your first job. An education will help you keep it. More important, with an education from a Christian perspective you will know why you are working in the first place. Therefore, choose your profession or the direction of your postgraduate life with kingdom values in mind.

The Special Demands on Christian Students

If these eighteen suggestions seem overwhelming, you have caught on to the fact that being a Christian student is very demanding—more demanding than just being a student. To succeed in college, a mere student has only to do well in the terms laid down by the university— its faculty and administration. To succeed as a Christian student, you have to do all that plus consider the whole enterprise from a Christian perspective. You have to develop not just an educated mind but an educated Christian mind.

For this reason you may find it impossible to get your normal college education in just four years. So? Take five or six.

In fact, I recommend taking a year or two just to study the Christian faith in relation to your intended profession. A number of Christian colleges and graduate schools have programs designed to link secular education and the marketplace. Two outstanding ones are New College Berkeley (California) and Regent College (Vancouver, B.C.). A year or two spent in directly studying the Christian faith in relation to the surrounding culture will make a major difference in your effectiveness as a Christian in the ordinary working or academic worlds.

Notes

Chapter 1: The Christian Mind

[1]Philippians 2:5.

[2]1 Corinthians 2:16.

[3]Harry Blamires, *The Christian Mind* (Ann Arbor: Servant, 1963), p. 43.

[4]William Wordsworth, "Lines Composed a Few Miles above Tintern Abbey," lines 68-70, frequently anthologized.

[5]Annie Dillard, *An American Childhood* (New York: Harper and Row, 1987), p. 125.

[6]William Wordsworth, *The Prelude*, I, ll. 356-400.

[7]Derek Kidner, *Proverbs* (Downers Grove, Ill.: InterVarsity Press, 1964), p. 59.

[8]D. A. Hubbard, "Wisdom," *The New Bible Dictionary* (Grand Rapids: Eerdmans, 1962), p. 1333. Ronald E. Murphy in "Wisdom," *Harper's Dictionary* (San Francisco, 1985), p. 1135, says Hebrew wisdom involved "the practical skill of coping with life (Prov 1:5; 11:14), and the pursuit of a life of proper ethical conduct (Prov 2:9-11 and throughout)."

[9]William Barclay puts it this way: "Jesus is the exact demonstration of what God is like, of the mind of God, of the attitude of God to man. In Jesus we see one who fed the hungry, healed the sick, comforted the sorrowing, was the friend of outcasts and sinners. And, because Jesus is one with God, he is the guarantee that God is like that." See *Jesus as They Saw Him* (Grand Rapids: Eerdmans, 1978), p. 333.

[10]Heraclitus, Fragment 60, in Kathleen Freeman, *Ancilla to the Pre-Socratic Phi-*

losophers (Cambridge, Mass.: Harvard University Press, 1957), p. 29.

[11]John Howard Yoder, *The Politics of Jesus* (Grand Rapids: Eerdmans, 1972), pp. 97-98.

[12]For a careful explanation of this passage see Gordon D. Fee, *The First Epistle to the Corinthians,* The New International Commentary on the New Testament (Grand Rapids: Eerdmans, 1987), pp. 27-120, esp. p. 120. For a refutation of the anti-intellectual interpretations of the passage, see Ranald Macaulay and Jerram Barrs, *Being Human* (Downers Grove, Ill.: InterVarsity Press, 1978), pp. 148-53.

[13]Czeslaw Milosz, *The Captive Mind* (New York: Vintage, 1953), p. 3.

[14]Alfred, Lord Tennyson, "Prologue" to *In Memoriam A. H. H.,* ll. 17-20.

[15]Lesslie Newbigin, *Foolishness to the Greeks* (Grand Rapids: Eerdmans, 1986), p. 60.

[16]David Edwards and John Stott, *Evangelical Essentials* (Downers Grove, Ill.: InterVarsity Press, 1989), p. 37.

[17]Os Guinness, "Knowing Means Doing: A Challenge to Think Christianly," *Radix* 18, no. 1 (1987).

[18]Much of what I have learned about sociological analysis comes by way of such Christian sociologists as Os Guinness, David Lyon, Robert N. Bellah and Tony Walter. See especially, Os Guinness, *The Gravedigger File* (Downers Grove, Ill.: InterVarsity Press, 1983); David Lyon, *Sociology and the Human Image* (Downers Grove, Ill.: InterVarsity Press, 1983) and *The Steeple's Shadow* (Grand Rapids: Eerdmans, 1985); Robert N. Bellah and others, *Habits of the Heart* (New York: Harper and Row, 1985); and Tony Walter, *Need: The New Religion* (Downers Grove, Ill.: InterVarsity Press, 1985). See also Stephen D. Eyre's *Defeating the Dragons of the World* (Downers Grove, Ill.: InterVarsity Press, 1987), which applies some of the insights of sociological analysis to ordinary Christian living.

Chapter 2: Mental Models of the World

[1]Alvin Toffler, *Future Shock* (New York: Bantam, 1971), p. 155.

[2]I trust those who have read my book *The Universe Next Door* will forgive the similar and sometimes identical phrasing of this definition of and the present introduction to *world views.* This particular formulation comes from the second edition of that book and is quite simply the best I can do at this point. See *The Universe Next Door,* 2d ed. (Downers Grove, Ill.: InterVarsity Press, 1988), p. 17. For a history and general examination of the concept of *world view* see Paul A. Marshall, Sander Griffioen and Richard J. Mouw, eds.,

Stained Glass: Worldviews and Social Science (Lanham, Md.: University Press of America, 1989); see especially James H. Olthuis's essay "On Worldviews," pp. 26-40 (which I read after writing the present chapter), which presents views virtually identical to my own.

³A. N. Whitehead, *Science and the Modern World* (New York: Mentor Books, 1948; first published in 1925), p. 49.

Chapter 3: The Final Reality

¹Satirizing our frustration in dealing with ultimate questions, Douglas Adams comments in his science fiction novel, "Capital letters were always the best way of dealing with things you didn't have a good answer to" *(Dirk Gently's Holistic Detective Agency* [New York: Pocket Books, 1987], p. 41).

²To have the father answer this way commits him to a Newtonian view of the world. We could have him answer in a more Einsteinian way that gravity is "a geometric effect, a curvature or warp in space-time. In this view, the earth remains in orbit simply because it is caught in the indentation our massive sun makes in space." (See Marcia Bartusiak, "What Place for a Creator?" a review of Stephen W. Hawking, *A Brief History of Time* (New York: Bantam, 1988) in *The New York Times Book Review* [April 3, 1988], p. 10). Timothy Ferris similarly says, "What we call gravitation is but the acceleration of objects as they slide down the toboggan runs described by their trajectories in time through the undulations of space. The planets skid along the inner walls of a depression in space created by the fat, massive sun; galaxies rest in spatial hollows like nuggets in a prospector's bowl" (quoted by Marcia Bartusiak, in a review of Timothy Ferris, *Coming of Age in the Milky Way* [New York: William Morrow, 1988 in *The New York Times Book Review* [July 17, 1988], pp. 28-29). But changing the father's answer to more modern physics would not change the outcome of the story. There are still only two possible choices: either the universe is the way it is (however one views gravity) simply because it is that way on its own (naturalism), or the universe is the way it is because something or some person brought it into existence (theism).

If some "thing" (nonperson) brought into being an orderly cosmos, it must have done so either from itself (in which case that "thing" is simply the cosmos in another form [in which case we have a naturalistic presupposition] or by a creative process totally gratuitous without intention (in which case the orderly universe is predicated on a pre-cosmic accident—a wrinkle in a vacuum [one is forced to use an irrational analogy]). In the latter case the universe is absurd at its core; we could say it was a hoax, except that it takes persons to play hoaxes. The alternative is that a "person" brought the world into being (which is the presupposition of theism).

[3]Carl Sagan, *Cosmos* (New York: Random House, 1980), p. 4.

[4]Charles E. Hummel, *The Galileo Connection* (Downers Grove, Ill.: InterVarsity Press, 1986), p. 57.

[5]This definition and the ensuing discussion is similar to the material on pages 26-28 of *The Universe Next Door.*

[6]The Westminster Confession, II, 1. For a consideration of the theistic concept of God from the standpoint of academic philosophy, see H. P. Owen, *Concepts of Deity* (London: Macmillan, 1971), pp. 1-48. Other metaphysical issues dealt with here are discussed in William Hasker, *Metaphysics* (Downers Grove, Ill.: InterVarsity Press, 1983); and C. Stephen Evans, *Philosophy of Religion* (Downers Grove, Ill.: InterVarsity Press, 1985).

[7]Geoffrey W. Bromiley, "The Trinity," *Baker's Dictionary of Theology* (Grand Rapids: Baker Book House, 1960), p. 531.

[8]From a private conversation July 1, 1988; the concept is being developed in a forthcoming book. Society has, of course, an important influence on our beliefs. Czelaw Milosz, commenting about the gradual movement of Eastern communist-bloc countries from general humanist and Christian world views to communism, says, "The greater the number of people who 'participate in culture'—i.e., pass through the schools, read books and magazines, attend theaters and exhibitions—the further the doctrine reaches and the smaller grows the threat to the rule of philosophers" (by which he means any one who really thinks about what they believe—*The Captive Mind,* trans. Jane Zielonko [New York: Vintage Books, 1955], p. 193). In parallel fashion our views are shaped by television, the schools and the general climate of thought in our communities. See chapter nine, pp. 174-77, below for a discussion of television in particular.

[9]Chapter ten below discusses in more detail the academic side of thinking worldviewishly.

[10]J. E. Lovelock, *Gaia: A New Look at Life on Earth* (Oxford: Oxford University Press, 1979). Lovelock himself should probably not, on the basis of this book, be called a pantheist. He grants no specific divinity at all to the earth or the cosmos. In fact, he apologizes for even using the personal pronoun *she* when he talks about Gaia: "I have frequently used the word Gaia as a shorthand for the hypothesis itself, namely that the biosphere is a self-regulating entity with the capacity to keep our planet healthy by controlling

the chemical and physical environment. Occasionally it has been difficult, without excessive circumlocution, to avoid talking of Gaia as if she were known to be sentient. This is meant no more seriously than is the appellation 'she' when given to a ship by those who sail in her, as a recognition that even pieces of wood and metal when specifically designed and assembled may achieve a composite identity with its own characteristic signature, as distinct from being the mere sum of its parts" (pp. ix-x). But later he grants a sort of sentience to Gaia: "If Gaia exists, then she is without a doubt intelligent in [a] limited sense at the least. There is a spectrum of intelligence ranging from the most rudimentary . . . to our own conscious and unconscious thoughts during the solving of a difficult problem" (p. 146). More than the beginnings of an Earth-mind thus seem an inevitable corollary to the Gaia hypothesis.

[11] Lewis Thomas, *Lives of a Cell* (New York: Bantam, 1975), p. 4.

[12] Lewis Thomas, "On the Uncertainty of Science," *The Harvard Magazine*, September/October, 1980, pp. 19-22. Phi Beta Kappa lecture, Harvard, 1980.

[13] Thomas, *Lives of a Cell*, p. 61.

[14] Hummel, *Galileo Connection*, p. 159. For an extended analysis of how Christianity in the Renaissance sparked scientific development, see R. Hooykaas, *Religion and the Rise of Modern Science* (Grand Rapids: Eerdmans, 1978). Lesslie Newbigin, *Foolishness to the Greeks,* pp. 69-72, also comments helpfully on rationality and contingency as key concepts in the founding of modern science.

[15] Three books on miracles are especially helpful. On a basic level is C. S. Lewis, *Miracles* (New York: Macmillan, 1947); on a more academic level are Richard Swinburne, *The Concept of Miracle* (New York: St. Martins, 1970), and Colin Brown, *Miracles and the Critical Mind* (Grand Rapids, Mich.: Eerdmans, 1984).

Chapter 4: The Riddle of the World

[1] Quoted in Michael Grant, *Myths of the Greeks and Romans* (New York: New American Library, 1964), p. 196.

[2] Loren Eisley, *The Unexpected Universe* (New York: Harcourt Brace Jovanovich, 1969), pp. 36-37.

[3] Ibid., pp. 41, 45.

[4] I am using the NIV marginal reading of verse 5 ("a little lower than God," the reading chosen by the RSV translators). The main text of the NIV reads, "a little lower than the heavenly beings."

[5]Robert Bellah and his colleagues at the University of California—Berkeley have written a major sociological study of individualism in America under this title, a phrase which they borrow from Alexis de Tocqueville's study in 1830, *Democracy in America*. See Robert Bellah and others, *Habits of the Heart* (San Francisco: Harper and Row, 1985), p. vii.

[6]Bellah, *Habits*, p. 143.

[7]Ibid., p. 33.

[8]Ibid., p. 35.

[9]Ibid., p. 34.

[10]Ibid.

[11]West Coast literature could provide a host of other examples from the work of such poets as Robinson Jeffers, Gary Snyder, Kenneth Rexroth and poetry of the beat generation.

[12]Bellah, *Habits*, p. 220.

[13]Ibid., p. 221.

[14]Quoted in Bruce Milne, *We Belong Together* (Downers Grove, Ill.: InterVarsity Press, 1978), p. 18.

[15]Both RSV's and NIV's *in* you fail to grasp the proper emphasis on community; see Ralph P. Martin, *The Epistle of Paul to the Philippians*, Tyndale New Testament Commentaries (Grand Rapids, Mich.: Eerdmans, 1959), p. 112.

[16]Karl Barth, *The Faith of the Church*, ed. Jean-Louis Leuba, trans. Gabriel Vahanian (New York: Meridian, 1958), p. 27.

[17]James Boswell, *The Life of Samuel Johnson*, ed. Edmund Fuller (New York: Dell, 1960), p. 155; see also pp. 235-36.

[18]Thomas, *The Lives of a Cell*, pp. 60-61.

[19]For some interesting Christian speculation on what heaven is like, see Peter Kreeft, *Everything You Ever Wanted to Know about Heaven But Never Dreamed of Asking* (San Francisco: Harper and Row, 1982).

[20]William Shakespeare, *Hamlet*, II, ii, 315-22.

[21]*Pascal's Pensées* (New York: E. P. Dutton, 1958), p. 121. Pensée No. 434.

Chapter 5: The Christian Mind as Mind

[1]From *A Source Book in Chinese Philosophy*, trans. Wing-tsit Chan (Princeton: Princeton University Press, 1963), p. 190.

[2]Os Guinness, *In Two Minds* (Downers Grove, Ill.: InterVarsity Press, 1976), p. 41.

[3]Stanley L. Jaki remarks, "Modern philosophy is caught . . . in a hapless oscillation between two extremes: the mirage of absolute certainty and utter

skepticism" *(Cosmos and Creator* [Chicago: Regnery Gateway, 1980], p. 141). See also C. S. Lewis's argument that "Nature is quite powerless to produce rational thought: not that she never modifies our thinking but that the moment she does so, it ceases (for that very reason) to be rational" *(Miracles* [London: Collins, 1961), p. 30).

⁴*Source Book in Chinese Philosophy,* pp. 190-91.

⁵Ibid., p. 183. Wing-tsit Chan notes that Chuang Chou's "spirit of doubt has contributed substantially to China's long tradition of skepticism" (ibid., p. 188). He also notes the charge of quietism laid against Chuang Chou by Confusionists. Chu Hsi (1130-1200), for example, said, "Lao Tzu still wanted to do something, but Chuang [Chou] did not want to do anything at all. He even said that he knew what to do but just did not want to do it" (ibid., p. 178).

⁶Samuel McCracken, "The Drugs of Habit and the Drugs of Belief," *Commentary* (June 1971), p. 49.

⁷Guinness, *In Two Minds,* p. 41.

⁸*Pascal's Pensées,* p. 121. Pensée No. 434.

⁹I believe that a Christian epistemology can best be framed by starting with *ontology. What is* is prior to *what can be known,* for knowing itself implies the existence of a knower and something to be known. So ontology precedes epistemology. Such was the grasp of philosophers up to René Descartes (1596-1650) who reversed the field and declared knowing to be philosophically prior to existence. His famous *cogito ergo sum* (I think; therefore I am) rested the very existence of the thinker on the process of thought. Some intellectual historians see in this the origin of today's subjectivism, relativism and general feeling that the world is not a solid place but one that itself is subject to definition and redefinition by every conscious human being. I tend to agree with this analysis and urge a return to the priority of being in philosophic pondering.

¹⁰Leon Morris, *The Gospel according to John* (Grand Rapids: Eerdmans, 1971), p. 115. See Leon Morris's extended commentary on the concept of the Logos, ibid., pp. 115-26. Also see Raymond Brown, *The Gospel according to John* (I-XII), Anchor Bible, vol. 29 (Garden City: Doubleday, 1966), pp. 519-24; C. H. Dodd, *The Interpretation of the Fourth Gospel* (Cambridge: University Press, 1968), pp. 263-85; A. Debrunner, H. Kleinknecht and G. Kittel, "λέγω," *Theological Dictionary of the New Testament,* 10 vols., ed. Gerhard Kittel and Gerhard Friedrich, trans. G. W. Bromiley (Grand Rapids: Eerdmans, 1964-76), 4:69-136; Gerhard Fries and Bertold Klappert, "Word, λόγος," *The New*

International Dictionary of New Testament Theology, ed. Colin Brown, 3 vols. (Grand Rapids; Zondervan, 1975-78), 3:1081-1117; Arthur F. Holmes, *All Truth is God's Truth* (Downers Grove, Ill.: InterVarsity Press, 1977), pp. 12-14. The exact meaning of *Logos* in the context of John's Gospel has been the subject of much speculation; it is probably safe to say that the issue is not resolved. My discussion focuses on what I see as the epistemological character of the *Logos,* its function as the foundation of all meaning, thereby undergirding as well the validity of John's argument that Jesus is the Christ.

[11]Morris, *Gospel according to John,* p. 116.

[12]Ibid., p. 116.

[13]John Marsh in *The Gospel of Saint John* (Baltimore: Penguin, 1968), p. 97, comments that the prolog sees "the Logos as the satisfying rational principle for understanding the universe. The Word may thus be likened to the eternal purpose of God, giving meaning to the whole of existence."

[14]I owe the origin of much of the thinking of the entire section on Ground Zero to a lecture given by C. Stephen Board, then on staff with InterVarsity Christian Fellowship, now managing director of Harold Shaw Publishing. He spoke on the opening verses of John 1, using the sentence that stuck in my mind like Br'er Rabbit to the tar baby: "Meaning is intrinsic to reality."

[15]As Marsh says, "Light was the first gift of creation, and here [Jn 1:4] the evangelist is stating that all the light of the world that brings insight and understanding to men is the work, the presence, of the Logos" *(Gospel of Saint John,* p. 104).

[16]William Barclay, *Jesus As They Saw Him* (Grand Rapids: Eerdmans, 1978), p. 427.

[17]Calvin *Institutes* 2.2.15.

[18]Ibid.

Chapter 6: The Discipleship of the Mind

[1]Os Guinness, "The Responsibility of Knowledge," *Radix* 18, no.1 (1987):28.

[2]Alasdair MacIntyre, *After Virtue,* 2d ed, (Notre Dame: Univ. of Notre Dame Press, 1984), p. 61.

[3]Allan Bloom begins his trenchant criticism of modern university education this way: "There is one thing a professor can be absolutely certain of: almost every student entering the university believes, or says he believes, that truth is relative. If this belief is put to the test, one can count on the students' reaction: they will be uncomprehending. That anyone should regard the proposition as not self-evident astonishes them, as though he were calling

into question 2 + 2 = 4. These are things you don't think about" *(The Closing of the American Mind* [New York: Simon and Schuster, 1987], p. 25). In other words, everything is relative except the statement that truth is relative.

⁴Alasdair MacIntyre tells the story of this movement in *After Virtue;* see especially pp. 57-59 and 83-84.

⁵Albert Camus opens *The Myth of Sisyphus,* trans. Justin O'Brien (New York: Vintage, 1960), p. 3, with this sentence: "There is but one truly serious philosophical problem, and that is suicide."

⁶Newbigin, *Foolishness to the Greeks,* p. 41.

⁷See, for example, David L. Wolfe, *Epistemology: the Justification of Belief* (Downers Grove, Ill.: InterVarsity Press, 1982).

⁸I have adapted an illustration from Francis Schaeffer, *He Is There and He Is Not Silent* in *The Complete Works of Francis Schaeffer,* 5 vols. (Westchester, Ill.: Crossway Books, 1982), 5:351-52.

⁹This long discourse is interrupted by the story of the woman taken in adultery; but this story seems to have been inserted into the narrative by a late editor. As a NIV marginal note says, "The earliest and most reliable manuscripts do not have John 7:53-8:11." With these verses removed, John 7—8 reads as one continuous narrative.

¹⁰Rebecca Manley Pippert, *Out of the Saltshaker* (Downers Grove, Ill.: InterVarsity Press, 1979), pp. 97-100.

Chapter 7: Getting to Know the Good

¹Saint-Exupéry, *Night Flight,* as quoted by Samuel C. Florman, *The Existential Pleasures of Engineering* (New York: St. Martin's Press, 1976), p. 139.

²*A Source Book in Chinese Philosophy,* p. 183.

³Shirley MacLaine, *Dancing in the Light* (New York: Bantam, 1985), p. 342.

⁴See discussion of the fact/value dichotomy, pp. 101-104 in chapter six above.

⁵Jacques Monod, *Chance and Necessity,* trans. Austryn Wainhouse (New York: Alfred A. Knopf, 1971), pp. 98 and 112.

⁶There are multitudes of long books written to help people read and interpret the Bible. Among them I recommend Norton Sterrett, *How to Understand Your Bible,* rev. ed. (Downers Grove, Ill.: InterVarsity Press, 1974); R. C. Sproul, *Knowing Scripture* (Downers Grove, Ill.: InterVarsity Press, 1977); A. J. Conyers, *How to Read the Bible* (Downers Grove, Ill.: InterVarsity Press, 1986); Joel Green, *How to Read the Gospels and Acts* (Downers Grove, Ill.: InterVarsity Press, 1987); Joel Green, *How to Read Prophecy* (Downers Grove, Ill.: InterVarsity Press, 1984); and Tremper Longman, *How to Read the Psalms*

(Downers Grove, Ill.: InterVarsity Press, 1988).

[7]Jacques Ellul, *The Technological Society*, trans. John Wilkinson (New York: Vintage, 1964), p. xxv.

[8]Brian J. Walsh and J. Richard Middleton, *The Transforming Vision* (Downers Grove, Ill.: InterVarsity Press, 1984), pp. 203-14.

[9]Langdon Winner, *The Whale and the Reactor: A Search for Limits in an Age of High Technology* (Chicago: Univ. of Chicago Press, 1986), p. 26. See also Mark Kramer, "The Ruination of the Tomato," *Atlantic Monthly*, January 1980, pp. 72-77; Peter Schrag, "Rubber Tomatoes: The Unsavory Partnership of Research and Agribusiness," *Harper's*, June 1978, pp. 24-29; and Marjorie Sun, "Weighing the Social Costs of Innovation," *Science*, March 30, 1984, pp. 1368-69.

[10]Winner, *The Whale and the Reactor*, p. 26.

[11]Personal interview with Alan Slade, professor of organizational psychology at the University of Delaware, who is my informant here.

[12]Ellul, *Technological Society*, p. xxv.

[13]Stephen V. Monsma et al., *Responsible Technology: A Christian Perspective* (Grand Rapids: Eerdmans, 1986), p. 3.

[14]Ibid.

[15]Winner, *The Whale and the Reactor*, p. 6.

[16]Alan Jiggins, *Human Future?* (London: Scripture Union, 1988), p. 94.

[17]Monsma, *Responsible Technology*, p. 32.

[18]Ibid., pp. 158-59, referring to Langdon Winner, *Autonomous Technology* (Cambridge: MIT Press, 1977), p. 100.

[19]Florman, *Existential Pleasures of Engineering*, p. 33.

[20]Carl Mitcham reports on Turkle's work in "Computer Ethos, Computer Ethics," *Research in Philosophy and Technology*, vol. 8 (Greenwich, Conn: JAI Press), p. 271.

[21]Ibid., p. 272.

[22]J. David Bolter says, "A defining technology defines or redefines man's role in relation to nature. By promising (or threatening) to replace man, the computer is giving us a new definition of man, as an 'information processor,' and of nature, as 'information to be processed' " (*Turing's Man*, p. 13, as quoted in ibid., p. 273). See also the much fuller treatment of these issues in Allen Emerson and Cheryl Forbes, *The Invasion of the Computer Culture* (Downers Grove, Ill.: InterVarsity Press, 1989), esp. pp. 80-105.

[23]Monsma, *Responsible Technology*, p. 49.

[24]Florman, *Existential Pleasures of Engineering*, p. 130.

[25]Ibid., p. 133.

[26]Ibid., p. 130-31.

[27]Monsma, *Responsible Technology*, p. 50.

[28]Ibid., p. 49, quoting Hans Jonas, "Toward a Philosophy of Technology," *Hastings Center Report*, February, 1979, p. 38.

[29]Mary Shelley, *Frankenstein* (New York: New American Library, 1963), p. 15.

[30]Ibid., p. 26.

[31]For a generally Christian approach to ecological issues, tending toward the placement of limits on technology, see the title essay in Wendell Berry, *The Gift of Good Land* (Berkeley: North Point Press, 1981), pp. 267-81; and Francis A. Schaeffer, *Pollution and the Death of Man* (Wheaton: Tyndale House, 1969). Both are responding to an influential essay by Lynn White, Jr., "The Historical Roots of Our Ecological Crisis" that puts Genesis 1:28 at the heart of the problem; Berry quotes White as saying, "Christianity . . . insisted that it is God's will that man exploit nature for his proper ends" (p. 269). Both Berry and Schaeffer show this to be a distorted interpretation of the Bible and Christian theology. See also the books on technology listed in Walsh and Middleton's bibliography (pp. 226-27).

[32]Monsma, *Responsible Technology*, pp. 39-40.

[33]Ibid., p. 19.

[34]Ibid., p. 40.

[35]Ibid., p. 68.

[36]Ibid., pp. 71-75.

[37]Ibid., p. 6; here the Calvin Center scholars refer readers to Nicholas Wolterstorff, *Until Justice and Peace Embrace* (Grand Rapids: Eerdmans, 1983), p. 70.

Chapter 8: Getting to Know the World

[1]John Henry Cardinal Newman, *The Idea of a University* in *English Prose of the Victorian Era*, ed. Charles Frederick Harrold and William D. Templeman (New York: Oxford University Press, 1938), pp. 593-94.

[2]One of the best books to put this aspect of knowing God in perspective is James Houston, *I Believe in the Creator* (Grand Rapids: Eerdmans, 1980).

[3]John R. W. Stott looks optimistically toward "an increasing integration of word and world, Scripture and nature, theology and science. It will involve what I have sometimes called the pain of 'double listening', as we listen above all to the word of God, although in the light of contemporary questions and opinions, but also to the voices of the modern world, although in submission to God's word" (David L. Edwards with John Stott, *Evangelical*

Essentials [Downers Grove, Ill.: InterVarsity Press, 1988], p. 335).

⁴This is in contrast to naturalism which posits a uniformity of natural causes in a closed system—that is, a system which cannot be affected from the outside since no such outside is thought to exist.

⁵Alfred North Whitehead, *Science and the Modern World* (New York: New American Library, 1948; first published, 1925), p. 4: "There can be no living science unless there is a widespread instinctive conviction in the existence of an *Order of Things*, and, in particular, of an *Order of Nature*. I have used the word *instinctive* advisedly. It does not matter what men say in words, so long as their activities are controlled by settled instincts."

⁶Hummel, *Galileo Connection*, p. 64.

⁷Many biblical scholars even in the nineteenth century did not believe Darwin's theories conflicted with the Bible. See Hummel, *Galileo Connection*, pp. 229-34; and James R. Moore, *The Post-Darwinian Controversies: A Study of the Protestant Struggle to Come to Terms with Darwin in Great Britain and America* (Cambridge: Cambridge University Press, 1979).

⁸Duane Thurman's *How to Think about Evolution* (Downers Grove, Ill.: InterVarsity Press, 1978) is somewhat dated but has an excellent approach to the subject. See also Hummel, *Galileo Connection*, pp. 223-66. Other books are listed in the biology section of the bibliography at the back of this book.

⁹Hummel, *Galileo Connection*, pp. 39-148. See as well the more philosophical treatment in R. Hooykaas, *Religion and the Rise of Modern Science* (Grand Rapids: Eerdmans, 1972).

¹⁰Whitehead, *Science and the Modern World*, p. 13.

¹¹Mary Stewart Van Leeuwen, *The Sorcerer's Apprentice* (Downers Grove, Ill.: InterVarsity Press, 1982), pp. 15-49, outlines the basically naturalist underpinnings of modern psychology.

¹²Sagan, *Cosmos*, p. 4.

¹³Van Leeuwen, *Sorcerer's Apprentice*, p. 44. A graduate student at Miami University told me recently that she tested in the "dogmatic" category in a test considered standard in the field of rhetoric. Apparently the main reason was that she believes that religious statements can be considered under the category of true or false.

¹⁴Ibid., quoting Paul Vitz, *Psychology as Religion: The Cult of Self-Worship* (Grand Rapids: Eerdmans, 1977), pp. 11-12.

¹⁵Calvin *Institutes* 2.2.12.

¹⁶Ibid.

¹⁷Ibid., 2.2.18.

[18]Ibid., 2.2.13-17.

[19]Ibid., 2.2.15.

[20]See D. Gareth Jones, *Brave New People*, rev. ed. (Grand Rapids: Eerdmans, 1985), especially chapters 4-5, pp. 78-149.

[21]Mary Stewart Van Leeuwen, "Between Reductionism and Self-Deification: The Challenge of the Cognitive Revival," *Center Journal*, Spring 1985, pp. 39-69, reprinted from *The Person in Psychology* (Grand Rapids: Eerdmans, 1985). See as well the remarkably insightful collection of essays edited by Thomas J. Burke, *Man and the Mind: A Christian Theory of Personality* (Hillsdale, Mich.: Hillsdale College Press, 1987); Mary Vander Goot's paper in this volume, "Has Modern Psychology Secularized Religion?" pp. 43-64, examines the fundamental naturalism of both Jean Piaget and Sigmund Freud.

[22]Mary Stewart Van Leeuwen, "Personality Theorizing within a Christian World View," in Burke, *Man and the Mind*, pp. 171-98; see as well Paul Vitz, "A Christian Theory of Personality: Covenant Theory" in the same volume, pp. 199-222; and his "A Covenant Theory of Personality: A Theoretical Introduction" in Lynne Morris, ed., *The Christian Vision: Man in Society* (Hillsdale, Mich.: Hillsdale College Press, 1984), pp. 75-99.

[23]B. F. Skinner, *Beyond Freedom and Dignity* (New York: Alfred A. Knopf, 1971), p. 5.

[24]John Platt, "Beyond Freedom and Dignity: 'A Revolutionary Manifesto,' " *The Center Magazine*, March-April, 1972, p. 35. See Mark Cosgrove, *B. F. Skinner's Behaviorism: An Analysis* (Grand Rapids: Zondervan, 1982) for a fuller critique of Skinner's theories by a Christian psychologist.

[25]Ibid.

[26]Skinner, *Beyond Freedom and Dignity*, p. 211.

[27]T. George Harris, "All the World's a Box," *Psychology Today*, August 1971, p. 34. Harris remarks, "Because Skinner believes in environmental conditioning, he takes care in reporting his early life. His family was warm and stable, and much concerned about good behavior. 'I was taught to fear God, the police, and what people will think,' he recalls, and he suspects that his reaction may have led him to try proving that people don't think at all. . . . His father took him through the county jail to show him the punishment he would face if he were to develop a criminal mind. He was never whipped. Once when he used a bad word, his mother washed out his mouth with soap. Grandmother Skinner had him peer into the glowing coals of the parlor stove to gain a sense of hell." Nonetheless even after having what he called a mystical experience as an adolescent, he became "within a year

the atheist he is today."

[28]Skinner, *Beyond Freedom and Dignity*, p. 202.

[29]Ibid., p. 21.

[30]Ibid., p. 199.

[31]B. F. Skinner, *Walden Two* (New York: Macmillan, 1962; first published, 1948), p. 240. See also *Beyond Freedom and Dignity*, p. 209.

[32]There is in fact a self-contradiction in much social science. As Allan Bloom points out, "Freud says that men are motivated by desire for sex and power, but he did not apply those motives to explain his own science or his own scientific activity. But if he can be a true scientist, i.e., motivated by love of the truth, so can other men, and his description of their motives is thus morally flawed. Or if he is motivated by sex or power, he is not a scientist, and his science is only one means among many possible to attain those ends. This contradiction runs throughout the social sciences. They give an account of things that cannot possibly explain the conduct of their practitioners" (*The Closing of the American Mind* [New York: Simon and Schuster, 1987], pp. 203-4). See also Mortimer Adler, *Philosopher at Large* (New York: Macmillan, 1977), pp. 198-99.

[33]Ralph C. Underwager does this in "What's Beyond Freedom and Dignity," *The Scientist and Ethical Decision* (Downers Grove, Ill.: InterVarsity Press, 1973), pp. 131-46.

[34]Bruce Nicholls, *Contextualization: A Theology of Gospel and Culture* (Downers Grove, Ill.: InterVarsity Press, 1979), p. 7.

[35]The essays in Burke, *Man and Mind: A Christian Theory of Personality*, do exactly that.

[36]Newman, *Idea of a University*, p. 575.

[37]Ibid.

[38]Ibid., p. 593.

[39]Ibid., pp. 593-94.

[40]Ibid., p. 594.

Chapter 9: Getting to Know the World

[1]Annie Dillard, *An American Childhood* (New York: Harper and Row, 1987), pp. 67 and 69.

[2]Richard H. Niebuhr, *Christ and Culture* (New York: Harper and Row, 1951).

[3]From the "Preface to *The Nigger of the Narcissus*" frequently anthologized.

[4]James W. Sire, *How to Read Slowly*, 2d ed. (Wheaton: Harold Shaw, 1988); this was previously published as both *How to Read Slowly* (Downers Grove,

Ill.: InterVarsity Press, 1978) and *The Joy of Reading* (Portland: Multnomah Press, 1984).

⁵*The Poems of Gerard Manley Hopkins*, 4th ed. (London: Oxford University Press, 1967), p. 69.

⁶Those philosophically inclined will see in "Pied Beauty" a reflection of the age-old problem of the one and the many. If everything is so various, what holds all the variety together? How can there be so many forms of one thing, the being of external reality? Christian theism locates the answer in God himself who is both one and many (Triune).

⁷*Collected Poems of Thomas Hardy* (New York: Macmillan, 1953), p. 137.

⁸As translated in Makoto Ueda, *Matsuo Basho* (Tokyo: Kodansha International Ltd., 1982), p. 44.

⁹Quoted at least in part from memory. Sometimes the final line is translated "splash" or "plop," but the word in Japanese is not onomatopoetic.

¹⁰As Donald Keene puts it, there is in this poem an intersection between the "eternal component" and the "momentary, personified by the movement of the frog." He goes on to say, "Their intersection is the splash of the water. Formally interpreted, the eternal component is the perception of truth . . . [related to] the philosophy of Zen Buddhism, which taught . . . that enlightenment was to be gained by a sudden flash of intuition" (*Japanese Literature: An Introduction for Western Readers* [Tokyo: Charles E. Tuttle, 1955], p. 39). Makoto Ueda comments on several poems like "The Ancient Pond": "Characteristically, each centers on the merging of the temporal into the eternal, of the mutable into the indestructible, of the tiny and finite into the vast and infinite, out of which emerges a primeval lonely feeling shared by all things in this world" (*Matsuo Basho*, p. 52).

¹¹As translated in Keene, *Japanese Literature*, p. 40.

¹²As translated in Ueda, *Matsuo Basho*, p. 53.

¹³See Leland Ryken's brief comment on these theories in "The Contours of Christian Criticism," *Christianity and Literature*, Fall 1987, p. 24.

¹⁴Ibid., pp. 23-24.

¹⁵Ibid., p. 26. Ryken is quoting from Jonathan Culler, "A Critic Against the Christians," *TLS*, November 23, 1984, pp. 1327-28.

¹⁶Robert Alter, *The Pleasures of Reading in an Ideological Age* (New York: Simon and Schuster, 1989), p. 9. Traditionalist Allan Bloom also treats these literary theories as fads (*Closing of the American Mind*, p. 379). And Robert Kimball, in "The Contemporary Sophist," *The New Criterion*, October 1989, pp. 5-15, writes a stinging critique of Stanley Fish's theorizing as summed up in Fish's

Doing What Comes Naturally (Durham: Duke University Press, 1989). On the other hand, the graduate department of English at Duke University, headed by Stanley Fish, is emphasizing the new theories; and Carnegie Mellon University is introducing undergraduates to them. *The Chronicle of Higher Education* has chronicled the rise of deconstructionism and the rear-guard action of traditionalists (see, for example, the November 25, 1987, and August 3, 1988, issues).

[17]Ryken, "The Contours of Christian Criticism," pp. 23-37. Clarence Walhout's "Response," published immediately following Ryken's paper, provides a useful critique and balance; Walhout finds modern critical approaches less nihilistic than Ryken, and so sees more hope in forging an alliance with modern theory rather than creating a separate Christian interpretative community as Ryken suggests.

[18]Matthew Arnold, *Culture and Anarchy* (1869) in *English Prose of the Victorian Era*, ed. by Charles Frederick Harold and William D. Templeman (New York: Oxford University Press, 1938), p. 1119.

[19]Neil Postman, *Amusing Ourselves to Death* (New York: Penguin, 1986), p. 92.

[20]Ibid., p. 16.

[21]Ibid., p. 50.

[22]Ibid., p. 16.

[23]Ibid., p. 121.

Chapter 10: What's It All About?

[1]Karl Löwith, *Meaning in History* (Chicago: University of Chicago Press, 1949), p. 184.

[2]Ernest Nagel, "Naturalism Reconsidered," in *Essays in Philosophy*, ed. Houston Peterson (New York: Pocket Library, 1959), p. 496.

[3]Ibid.

[4]H. J. Blackham, "The Pointlessness of It All," *Objections to Humanism* (Harmondsworth: Penguin, 1965), p. 103.

[5]These are lines from a longer poem of unrelieved pessimism in *Fleurs du Mal*, trans. Richard Howard (Boston: David R. Godine, 1982), p. 155.

[6]Peter Craigie, *Word Biblical Commentary: Psalms 1-50*, vol. 19 (Waco, Tex.: Word Books, 1983), p. 68.

[7]Ibid., p. 69.

[8]Löwith, *Meaning in History*, pp. 183-84.

[9]See my discussion in *The Universe Next Door*, pp. 41-43.

[10]Annie Dillard, *An American Childhood*, p. 9.

[11]Newbigin, *Foolishness to the Greeks,* p. 124.

[12]John Howard Yoder, *The Politics of Jesus* (Grand Rapids: Eerdmans, 1972), p. 242.

[13]Ibid., p. 235.

[14]Jesus "is to be looked at as a mover of history and as the standard by which Christians must learn how they are to look at the moving of history" (ibid., 239).

[15]Ibid., pp. 97-98. Because this is a somewhat controversial way to interpret the implications of the cross, I will let Yoder speak further for himself: "The universal testimony of Scripture is that Christians are those who follow Christ at just this point. . . . Philippians 2, was cited by the Apostle as part of his plea to the Christians at Philippi to live together more unselfishly. The visions of the book of Revelation go on from the heavenly throne room, where the Lamb is praised, to a vision of triumph (ch. 12) where the multitude of 'our brethren' has defeated the dragon 'by the blood of the lamb and by the word of their testimony, for they loved not their lives even unto death.' Elsewhere, Paul can describe the entire apostolic ministry with its inner and outer sufferings as a matter of 'carrying about in our bodies the putting to death of Jesus, so that in our bodies the life of Jesus also may be made manifest.' This is what Jesus himself meant by recognizing as a disciple only him who is ready to take up a cross and follow him" (ibid., p. 241). See also John R. W. Stott, *The Cross of Christ* (Downers Grove, Ill.: InterVarsity Press, 1986), pp. 289-94; and 318-26.

[16]Yoder, *Politics of Jesus,* p. 242.

Appendix: Thinking Your Way through College

[1]Stephen, speaking to the Sanhedrin, Acts 7:22.

[2]Daniel 1:3-4, 6.

[3]Annie Dillard, *Encounters with Chinese Writers* (Middletown, Conn.: Wesleyan University Press, 1984), p. 46.

A Bibliography We Can't Live Without
compiled by Brian J. Walsh and J. Richard Middleton

This bibliography is a revision of the one that first appeared in *The Transforming Vision: Shaping a Christian World View* (Downers Grove, Ill.: InterVarsity Press, 1984). As with that earlier version, we have made a deliberate attempt not to be comprehensive. In most of the fields listed, there are many more books than the ones we have included. Rather than writing a comprehensive bibliography, we have attempted to compile the "bibliography we can't live without." These books are the essentials. Although we do not necessarily endorse everything that all of these books say, we nevertheless believe them to be foundational to developing a Christian perspective in each discipline.

The bibliography has four sections: I. World Views and Cultural Analysis; II. Natural and Applied Sciences; III. The Humanities and Social Sciences; and IV. After School: Work and Leisure. Sections I and IV list resources with which everyone should be familiar. Sections II and III have subheadings for assorted disciplines offered at the university. Obviously, we all need to be reading the books in our own particular discipline.

We have also included a list of general books on "Forming a Christian Perspective in Science" and "Setting a Christian Foundation in the Humanities and Social Sciences" at the beginning of sections II and III respectively.

These books, together with those listed under "Christian Faith and University Study," are helpful in getting a broader Christian perspective in our studies, which then must be worked out more specifically in each student's discipline.

All of the books in this bibliography are important. They are gifts that the Lord has given to the Christian community to help it to grow in all things into Christ. But to help students choose the *most* important books, we have placed an asterisk (*) beside three or four entries under each subheading. The books in this bibliography are foundational. Once the foundation has been set, we must build on it. We will need to search out other resources to help us be Christian students, integrated and whole.

I. World Views and Cultural Analysis
What Are World Views?

Berger, Peter. *The Sacred Canopy: Elements of a Sociological Theory of Religion.* Garden City: Doubleday, 1967.

Holmes, Arthur. *Contours of a World View.* Grand Rapids, Mich.: Eerdmans, 1983.

Kraft, Charles. *Christianity in Culture.* Maryknoll, N.Y.: Orbis, 1979.

Marshall, Paul, et al. *Stained Glass: Worldviews and Social Science.* Christian Studies Today Series. Lanham, Md.: University Press of America, 1989.

Olthuis, James H. "On Worldviews." *Christian Scholar's Review* 14, 2 (1985):153-64.

*Sire, James W. *The Universe Next Door: A Basic World View Catalog.* 2d ed. Downers Grove, Ill.: InterVarsity Press, 1988.

Smart, Ninian. *Worldviews: Crosscultural Explorations of Human Beliefs.* New York: Charles Scribner's Sons, 1983.

Stevenson, Leslie. *Seven Theories of Human Nature.* New York: Oxford, 1974.

*Walsh, Brian J., and Middleton, J. Richard. *The Transforming Vision: Shaping a Christian Worldview.* Downers Grove, Ill.: InterVarsity Press, 1984.

Distinctives of the Christian World View

Blamires, Harry. *The Christian Mind.* Ann Arbor: Servant, 1978.

_____ . *Recovering the Christian Mind.* Downers Grove, Ill.: InterVarsity Press, 1988.

*Brueggemann, Walter. *The Prophetic Imagination.* Philadelphia: Fortress, 1978.

Ellul, Jacques. *The Presence of the Kingdom.* Translated by Olive Wyon. New York: Seabury Press, 1967.

Fernhout, Harry. *Of Kings and Prophets: A Study of the Book of Kings.* Toronto: Curriculum Development Centre, 1979.

_____ . *Promises Broken, Promise Kept: A Readers Guide to I and II Samuel.* Toronto: Curriculum Development Centre, 1986.

Hall, Douglas John. *Imaging God: Dominion as Stewardship.* Grand Rapids, Mich.: Eerdmans; New York: Friendship Press, 1986.

Ladd, George Eldon. *The Pattern of New Testament Truth.* Grand Rapids, Mich.: Eerdmans, 1968.

Mouw, Richard J. *Called to Holy Worldliness.* Philadelphia: Fortress, 1980.

*_____ . *When the Kings Come Marching In.* Grand Rapids, Mich.: Eerdmans, 1984.

*Niebuhr, H. Richard. *Christ and Culture.* New York: Harper & Row, 1983.

Noll, Mark, and Wells, David, eds. *Christian Faith and Practice in the Modern World.* Grand Rapids, Eerdmans, 1987.

Sinnema, Donald. *Reclaiming the Land: A Study of the Book of Joshua.* Teacher and Study Group Edition. Toronto: Curriculum Development Centre, 1977.

Wallis, Jim. *The Call to Conversion.* San Francisco: Harper & Row, 1981.

*Wolters, Albert. *Creation Regained: Biblical Basics for a Reformational Worldview.* Grand Rapids, Mich.: Eerdmans, 1985.

Christian Faith and University Study

Carpenter, Joel A., and Shipps, Kenneth W., eds. *Making Higher Education.* St. Paul: Christian University Press; Grand Rapids, Mich.: Eerdmans, 1987.

Gill, David. *The Opening of the Christian Mind.* Downers Grove, Ill.: InterVarsity Press, 1989.

*Heie, Harold, and Wolfe, David L., eds. *The Reality of Christian Learning: Strategies for Faith-Discipline Integration.* St. Paul: Christian University Press; Grand Rapids, Mich.: Eerdmans, 1987.

Holmes, Arthur. *All Truth Is God's Truth.* Downers Grove, Ill.: InterVarsity Press, 1977.

Malik, Charles. *A Christian Critique of the University.* Downers Grove, Ill.: InterVarsity Press, 1982.

Marsden, George. "The State of Evangelical Christian Scholarship." *Christian Scholar's Review* 17, 4 (1988): 347-60.

Sire, James W. *How to Read Slowly: A Guide to Reading with the Mind.* Wheaton, Ill.: Harold Shaw, 1988.

Stott, John. *Your Mind Matters.* Downers Grove, Ill.: InterVarsity Press, 1973.

Vieth, Gene Edward, Jr. *Loving God with All the Mind.* Westchester, Ill.: Crossway, 1987.

Wilkes, Peter, ed. *Christianity Challenges the University*. Downers Grove, Ill.: InterVarsity Press, 1981.

*Wolterstorff, Nicholas. *Reason within the Bounds of Religion*. 2d ed. Grand Rapids, Mich.: Eerdmans, 1984.

Further Resources:
Faculty Dialogue
Journal of the Institute for Christian Leadership
9733 S.E. Frence Acres Dr.
Portland, OR 97266-6911

Analysis of Western Culture

Barrett, William. *Death of the Soul: From Descartes to the Computer*. New York: Anchor Press, 1986.

Bellah, Robert, et al. *Habits of the Heart: Individualism and Commitment in American Life*. Berkeley: Univ. of California Press, 1985.

Berger, Peter. *Facing Up to Modernity: Excursions in Society, Religion and Politics*. New York: Basic Books, 1977.

Dooyeweerd, Herman. *Roots of Western Culture: Pagan, Secular, and Christian Options*. Translated by J. Kraay. Toronto: Wedge, 1979.

*Ellis, Carl, Jr. *Beyond Liberation: The Gospel and the Black American Experience*. Downers Grove, Ill.: InterVarsity Press, 1983.

Ellul, Jacques. *The Betrayal of the West*. New York: Seabury, 1978.

*Goudzwaard, Bob. *Capitalism and Progress: A Diagnosis of Western Society*. Translated by J. Van Nuis Zylstra. Grand Rapids, Mich.: Eerdmans, 1979.

*————. *Idols of Our Time*. Translated by Mark VanderVennen. Downers Grove, Ill.: InterVarsity Press, 1984.

Groothuis, Douglas. *Unmasking the New Age*. Downers Grove, Ill.: InterVarsity Press, 1986.

Guinness, Os. *The Gravedigger File: Papers on the Subversion of the Modern Church*. Downers Grove, Ill.: InterVarsity Press, 1983.

*Newbigin, Lesslie. *Foolishness to the Greeks: The Gospel and Western Culture*. Grand Rapids, Mich.: Eerdmans, 1986.

Walsh, Brian J. *Who Turned Out the Lights? The Light of the Gospel in a Post-Enlightenment Culture*. Toronto: Institute for Christian Studies, 1989.

Walter, Tony. *Need: The New Religion*. Downers Grove, Ill.: InterVarsity Press, 1985.

II. Natural and Applied Sciences
General Books on Forming a Christian Perspective in Science

*Barbour, Ian. *Issues in Science and Religion.* New York: Harper & Row, 1966.
_____ . *Myths, Models and Paradigms.* London: SCM, 1974.

Gerhart, Mary, and Russell, Allan. *Metaphoric Process: The Creation of Scientific and Religious Understanding.* Fort Worth, Tex.: Texas University Press, 1984.

*Gilkey, Langdon. *Religion and the Scientific Future: Reflections on Myth, Science, and Theology.* New York: Harper & Row, 1970. Reprint ed. Macon, Ga.: Mercer University Press, 1981.

Gutting, Gary, ed. *Paradigms and Revolutions: Applications and Appraisals of Thomas Kuhn's Philosophy of Science.* Notre Dame, Ind.: Univ. of Notre Dame Press, 1980.

*Hooykaas, R. *Religion and the Rise of Modern Science.* Grand Rapids, Mich.: Eerdmans, 1972.

Hummel, Charles. *The Galileo Connection: Resolving Conflicts between Science and the Bible.* Downers Grove, Ill.: InterVarsity Press, 1986.

Hyers, Conrad. *The Meaning of Creation: Genesis and Modern Science.* Atlanta: John Knox Press, 1984.

Joldersma, Clarence. *Beliefs and the Scientific Enterprise.* Toronto: Institute for Christian Studies, 1983.

Kuhn, Thomas S. *The Structure of Scientific Revolutions.* 2d ed. Chicago: Univ. of Chicago Press, 1970.

Lindberg, David C., and Numbers, Ronald C., eds. *God and Nature: Historical Essays on the Encounter between Christianity and Science.* Berkeley: Univ. of California Press, 1986.

MacKay, Donald. *The Clockwork Image.* Downers Grove, Ill.: InterVarsity Press, 1974.

Polanyi, Michael. *The Tacit Dimension.* Garden City: Doubleday, 1967.

*Ratzsch, Del. *Philosophy of Science: The Natural Sciences in Christian Perspective.* Downers Grove, Ill.: InterVarsity Press, 1986.

Russell, Colin A. *Cross-currents: Interactions between Science and Faith.* Grand Rapids, Mich.: Eerdmans, 1985.

Stafleu, Marinus Dirk. *Theories at Work.* Lanham, Md.: University Press of America, 1987.

Templeton, John, and Hermann, Robert. *The God Who Would Be Known: Divine Revelations in Contemporary Science.* San Francisco: Harper & Row, 1988.

*Van Till, Howard. *The Fourth Day: What the Bible and Heavens Are Telling Us* *about Creation.* Grand Rapids, Mich.: Eerdmans, 1986.

Further Resources:
Perspectives on Science and Christian Faith
Journal of the American Scientific Affiliation
P.O. Box 668
Ipswich, MA 01938

Science and Christian Belief
Journal of "Christians in Science" and "The Victo.ia Institute"
Paternoster Press
Paternoster House
3 Mount Radford Crescent
Exeter EX2 4JW
United Kingdom

Biology (and the evolution debate)

Frye, Roland M., ed. *Is God a Creationist?* New York: Charles Scribner's Sons, 1983.

*Gilkey, Langdon. *Creationism on Trial: Evolution and God at Little Rock.* Minneapolis: Winston Press, 1985.

Gillespie, Neal C. *Charles Darwin and the Problem of Creation.* Chicago: Univ. of Chicago Press, 1979.

*Greene, John C. *Science, Ideology and World View: Essays in the History of Evolutionary Ideas.* Berkeley: Univ. of California Press, 1981.

Price, David; Wiester, John; and Hearn, Walter R. *Teaching Science in a Climate of Controversey.* Ipswich, Mass.: American Scientific Affiliation, 1986.

Thurman, D. L. *How to Think about Evolution (and Other Bible-Science Controversies).* Downers Grove, Ill.: InterVarsity Press, 1978.

Wiester, John. *The Genesis Connection.* Nashville, Thomas Nelson, 1983.

*Wright, Richard T. *Biology through the Eyes of Faith.* San Francisco: Harper & Row, 1989.

Van Till, Howard, et al. *Science Held Hostage: What's Wrong with Creation Science* and *Evolutionism.* Downers Grove, Ill.: InterVarsity Press, 1988.

Geography and Environmental Studies

Austin, Richard Cartwright. *Hope for the Land: Nature in the Bible.* Atlanta: John Knox Press, 1988.

*Brueggemann, Walter. *The Land.* Overtures to Biblical Theology Series. Philadelphia: Fortress, 1977.

Carmody, John. *Ecology and Religion: Toward a New Christian Theology of Nature.* New York: Paulist Press, 1983.

Glacken, Clarence J. *Traces on the Rhodian Shore: Nature and Culture in Western Thought from Ancient Times to the End of the Eighteenth Century.* Berkeley: Univ. of California Press, 1976.

Granberg-Michaelson, Wesley, ed. *Tending the Garden: Essays on the Gospel and the Earth.* Grand Rapids, Mich.: Eerdmans, 1987.

*_____ . *A Worldly Spirituality: The Call to Redeem Life on Earth.* San Francisco: Harper & Row, 1984.

Passmore, John. *Man's Responsibility for Nature: Ecological Problems and Western Traditions.* London: Gerald Duckworth, 1974.

Santmire, Paul. *The Travail of Nature: The Ambiguous Ecological Promise of Christian Theology.* Philadelphia: Fortress, 1980.

Schaeffer, Francis. *Pollution and the Death of Man.* Wheaton, Ill.: Tyndale House, 1969.

*Wilkinson, Loren, et al. *Earthkeeping: Christian Stewardship of Natural Resources.* Grand Rapids, Mich.: Eerdmans, 1980.

Physical Sciences

Jaki, Stanley. *The Road of Science and the Ways of God.* Chicago: Univ. of Chicago Press, 1980.

MacKay, Donald, ed. *Christianity in a Mechanistic Universe.* Downers Grove, Ill.: InterVarsity Press, 1965.

*Owens Virginia Stem. *And the Trees Clap Their Hands: Faith, Perception and the New Physics.* Grand Rapids, Mich.: Eerdmans, 1983. Reprinted as *God Spy: Faith Perception and the New Physics.* Bellevue, Wash.: Alta Vista College Press, 1988.

Pollard, W. *Physicist and Christian.* Greenwich, Conn.: Seabury, 1961.

Russell, R. J.; Stoeger, W. R.; and Coyne, G. V. *Physics, Philosophy and Theology: A Common Quest for Understanding.* Notre Dame, Ind.: Univ. of Notre Dame Press, 1988.

Stafleu, Marinus Dirk. *Time and Again: A Systematic Analysis of the Foundations of Physics.* Toronto: Wedge, 1980.

*Van Till, Howard. *The Fourth Day: What the Bible and the Heavens Are Telling Us about Creation.* Grand Rapids, Mich.: Eerdmans, 1986.

Mathematics

Baker, T, and Jongsma, C. *The Shape and Number of Things*. Toronto: Curriculum Development Centre, 1981. (This is an exciting elementary school curriculum.)

*Brabenac, R. L., et al. *A Christian Perspective on the Foundations of Mathematics*. Wheaton, Ill.: Wheaton College, 1977.

Granville, H., Jr. *Logos: Mathematics and Christian Theology*. E. Brunswick, N.J.: Bucknell University Press, 1976.

Jongsma, Calvin. "Christianity and Mathematics: An Analysis of Differing Approaches to the Interrelationship." Toronto: Institute for Christian Studies Academic Paper Series, 1985.

Van Brummelen, Harro W. "The Place of Mathematics in the Curriculum." In *Shaping School Curriculum: A Biblical View*. Edited by G. Steensma. Terre Haute, Ind.: Signal Press, 1977.

Further Resources:
Bibliography of Christianity and Mathematics
Compiled by: Gene B. Chase and Calvin Jongsma
Sioux Center, Iowa: Dordt College Press, 1983

Technology Studies

Bolter, David J. *Turing's Man: Western Culture in a Computer Age*. Chapel Hill, N.C.: Univ. of North Carolina Press, 1984.

Dreyfus, Hubert L., and Dreyfus, Stuart E. *Mind over Machine: The Power of Human Expertise in the Era of the Computer*. New York: Free Press, 1986.

Ellul, Jacques. *The Technological Society*. New York: Random House, 1967.

Emerson, Allen, and Forbes, Cheryl. *The Invasion of the Computer Culture*. Downers Grove, Ill.: InterVarsity Press, 1989.

*Lyon, David. *The Silicon Society*. Grand Rapids, Mich.: Eerdmans, 1986.

Mitcham, Carl, and Grote, Tim. *Theology and Technology: Essays in Christian Analysis and Engineering*. Lanham, Md.: University Press of America, 1984.

*Monsma, Stephen, et al. *Responsible Technology*. Grand Rapids, Mich.: Eerdmans, 1986.

Rifkin, Jeremy. *Declarations of a Heretic*. Boston: Routledge and Kegan Paul, 1985.

————. *Time Wars: The Primary Conflict in Human History*. New York: Henry Holt, 1987.

Schumacher, E. F. *Small Is Beautiful*. New York: Harper & Row, 1976.

Schuurman, Egbert. *Technology and the Future.* Toronto: Wedge, 1980
_____ . *Reflections on the Technological Society.* Toronto: Wedge, 1977.
Winner, L. *The Whale and the Reactor: A Search for Limits in an Age of High Technology.* Chicago: Univ. of Chicago Press, 1986.

Medicine and Health Care

*Allen, David E.; Bird, Lewis P.; and Herrmann, Robert, eds. *Whole Person Medicine: An International Symposium.* Downers Grove, Il¹.: InterVarsity Press, 1980.
*Bouma, Hessel, et al. *Christian Faith, Health and Medical Practice.* Grand Rapids, Mich.: Eerdmans, 1989.
Granberg-Michaelson, Karin. *In the Land of the Living: Health Care and the Church.* Grand Rapids, Mich.: Zondervan, 1984.
Hauerwas, Stanley. *Suffering Presence: Theological Reflections on Medicine, the Mentally Handicapped and the Church.* Notre Dame, Ind.: Univ. of Notre Dame Press, 1986.
Jones, D. Gareth. *Our Fragile Brains.* Downers Grove, Ill.: InterVarsity Press, 1980.
*Kelsey, Morton. *Psychology, Medicine and Christian Healing.* San Francisco: Harper & Row, 1989.
Lammers, Stephen E., and Verhey, Allen, eds. *On Moral Medicine: Theological Perspectives in Medical Ethics.* Grand Rapids, Mich.: Eerdmans, 1987.
Marty, Martin, and Vaux, Kenneth, eds. *Health/Medicine and the Faith Traditions: An Inquiry into Religion and Medicine.* Philadelphia: Fortress, 1982.
Nelson, J. B. *Human Medicine.* Minneapolis: Augsburg, 1973.
Ramsey, Paul. *Fabricated Man.* New Haven, Conn.: Yale University Press, 1970.
Shelly, Judith Allen. *Dilemma: A Nurse's Guide for Making Ethical Decisions.* Downers Grove, Ill.: InterVarsity Press, 1980.
Shelly, Judith Allen, and Fish, Sharon. *Spiritual Care: The Nurse's Role.* 3d ed. Downers Grove, Ill.: InterVarsity Press, 1988.

Food and Agriculture

Berry, Wendell. *The Gift of Good Land.* Berkeley: North Point Press, 1981.
*_____ . *The Unsettling of America.* New York: Avon, 1978.
Freudenberger, C. Dean. *Food for Tomorrow.* Minneapolis: Augsburg, 1984.
Hightower, Jim. *Eat Your Heart Out: How Food Profiteers Victimize the Consumer.* New York: Crown, 1975.
Jackson, Wes. *New Roots for Agriculture.* Acton, Mass.: Brick House Publishing,

1980.

Jackson, Wes; Coleman, Bruce; and Berry, Wendell; eds. *Meeting the Expectations of the Land: Essays on Sustainable Agricultural Stewardship.* St. Louis, Mo.: North Point Press, 1985.

Lappé, Frances M., and Collins, Joseph. *Food First: Beyond the Myth of Scarcity.* New York: Ballantine, 1977.

*_____ . *World Hunger: Twelve Myths.* New York: Grove Books, 1986.

*Longacre, D. Janzen. *Living More with Less.* Scottdale, Pa.: Herald Press, 1980.

_____ . "Introduction." In *More-with-Less Cookbook.* Scottdale, Pa.: Herald Press, 1976.

Lutz, Charles. *Farming the Lord's Land: Christian Perspectives on American Agriculture.* Minneapolis: Augsburg, 1980.

McGinnis, J. *Bread and Justice.* Ramsey, N.J.: Paulist Press, 1979.

Nelson, J. A. *Hunger for Justice.* Maryknoll, N.Y.: Orbis, 1980.

Simon, Arthur. *Bread for the World.* Grand Rapids, Mich.: Eerdmans, 1975.

Voran, Marilyn Helmuth. *Add Justice to Your Shopping List: A Guide for Reshaping Your Food Buying Habits.* Scottdale, Pa.: Herald Press, 1986.

Further Resources:

Earthkeeping: A Quarterly on Faith and Agriculture
Published by the Christian Farmer's Federations of Ontario and Alberta
10766 - 97 St.
Edmonton, Alberta T5H 2M1
Canada

Note: Agriculture and nutrition students should also pay attention to books listed under "Geography and Environmental Studies" above.

III. The Humanities and Social Sciences
General Books Setting a Christian Foundation in the Humanities and Social Sciences

*Evans, C. Stephen. *Preserving the Person.* Downers Grove, Ill.: InterVarsity Press, 1973. Reprint ed. Grand Rapids, Mich.: Baker, 1982.

Gaede, S. D. *Where Gods May Dwell: Understanding the Human Condition.* Grand Rapids, Mich.: Zondervan, 1985.

Guinness, Os. *The Dust of Death.* Downers Grove, Ill.: InterVarsity Press, 1973.

Jeeves, Malcolm A., ed. *Behavioural Sciences: A Christian Perspective.* Leicester, U.K.: Inter-Varsity Press, 1988.

Lyon, David. *The Steeple's Shadow: On the Myths and Realities of Secularization.*

Grand Rapids, Mich.: Eerdmans, 1987.

*Marshall, Paul, and VanderVennen, Robert, eds. *Social Science in Christian Perspective.* Lanham, Md.: University Press of America, 1988.

Seerveld, Calvin. *On Being Human: Imaging God in the Modern World.* Burlington, Ont.: Welch Publishing Co., 1989.

Van Leeuwen, Mary Stewart. "North American Evangelicalism and the Social Sciences: A Historical and Critical Appraisal." *Perspectives on Science and Christian Faith* 40, 4 (December 1988):194-203.

*Wolterstorff, Nicholas. *Until Justice and Peace Embrace.* Grand Rapids, Mich.: Eerdmans, 1983.

Philosophy

Brown, Colin. *Christianity & Western Thought.* Vol 1: *From the Ancient World to the Age of Enlightenment.* Downers Grove, Ill.: InterVarsity Press, 1990.

Brown, Colin. *Philosophy and the Christian Faith.* Downers Grove, Ill.: InterVarsity Press, 1969.

Casserley, Langmead. *The Christian in Philosophy.* New York: Charles Scribner's Sons, 1951.

Dooyeweerd, Herman. *In the Twilight of Western Thought.* Nutley, N.J.: Craig Press, 1968.

Evans, C. Stephen. *Philosophy of Religion.* Downers Grove, Ill.: InterVarsity Press, 1982.

*Hart, Hendrik. *Understanding Our World: An Integral Ontology.* Lanham, Md.: University Press of America, 1984.

Holmes, Arthur. *Philosophy: A Christian Perspective.* Downers Grove, Ill.: InterVarsity Press, 1975.

McIntire, C. T., ed. *The Legacy of Herman Dooyeweerd.* Lanham, Md.: University Press of America, 1985.

Schouls, Peter A. *Descartes and the Enlightenment.* Kingston, Ont., and Montreal, PQ: McGill-Queens University Press, 1989.

_____. *The Imposition of Method: A Study of Descartes and Locke.* Oxford: Clarendon Press, 1980.

*Wolfe, David L. *Epistemology: The Justification of Belief.* Downers Grove, Ill.: InterVarsity Press, 1982.

*Wolters, Albert. *Our Place in the Philosophical Tradition.* Toronto: Institute for Christian Studies, 1975.

*Wolterstorff, Nicholas. *Reason within the Bounds of Religion.* 2d ed. Grand Rapids, Mich.: Eerdmans, 1984.

Yandell, Keith. *Christianity and Philosophy*. Grand Rapids: Eerdmans, 1984.

Further Resources:
Faith and Philosophy
Journal of the Society of Christian Philosophers
c/o Department of Philosophy
Asbury College
Wilmore, KY 40390

Biblical Studies
Anderson, Bernhard W. *Creation Versus Chaos: The Reinterpretation of Mythical Symbolism in the Bible*. New York: Association Press, 1967. Reprint ed. Philadelphia: Fortress, 1987.

Blomberg, Craig L. *The Historical Reliability of the Gospels*. Downers Grove, Ill.: InterVarsity Press, 1987.

Borg, Marcus. *Jesus: A New Vision*. San Francisco: Harper & Row, 1987.

Brueggemann, Walter. *Hopeful Imagination*. Philadelphia: Fortress, 1986.

*_____ . *Israel's Praise: Doxology Against Idolatry and Ideology*. Philadelphia: Fortress, 1988.

Childs, Brevard. *Introduction to the Old Testament as Scripture*. Philadelphia: Fortress, 1979.

*Hanson, Paul. *The People Called: The Growth of Community in the Bible*. San Francisco: Harper & Row, 1985.

Hasel, Gerhard. *Old Testament Theology: Basic Issues in the Current Debate*. Rev. ed. Grand Rapids, Mich.: Eerdmans, 1975.

_____ . *New Testament Theology: Basic Issues in the Current Debate*. Grand Rapids, Mich.: Eerdmans, 1978.

Ladd, George E. *The New Testament and Criticism*. Grand Rapids, Mich.: Eerdmans, 1966.

Marshall, I. Howard, ed. *New Testament Interpretation: Essays on Principles and Methods*. Exeter, U.K.: Paternoster; Grand Rapids, Mich.: Eerdmans, 1977.

*Neill, Stephen, and Wright, Tom. *The Interpretation of the New Testament: 1861—1986*. 2d ed. Oxford: Oxford University Press, 1988.

Noll, Mark. *Between Faith and Criticism*. San Francisco: Harper & Row, 1987.

Ridderbos, Herman. *Paul: An Outline of His Theology*. Translated by J. R. deWitt. Grand Rapids, Mich.: Eerdmans, 1975.

Seerveld, Calvin G. *Balaam's Apocalypic Prophecies: A Study in Reading Scripture*.

2d ed. Toronto: Wedge, 1980.

*Swartley, Willard. *Slavery, Sabbath, War, Women.* Scottdale, Pa.: Herald Press, 1983.

Theissen, Gerd. *The Shadow of the Galilean: The Quest of the Historical Jesus in Narrative Form.* Translated by John Bowden. London: SCM, 1987.

Wright, Christopher. *An Eye for an Eye: The Place of Old Testament Ethics Today.* Downers Grove, Ill.: InterVarsity Press, 1983.

Yoder, Perry. *From Word to Life: A Guide to the Art of Bible Study.* Scottdale, Pa.: Herald Press, 1982.

Theological Studies

*Berkhof, Hendrikus. *The Christian Faith.* Rev. ed. Translated by Sierd Woudstra. Grand Rapids, Mich.: Eerdmans, 1986.

Boesak, Alan. *Black and Reformed.* Maryknoll, N.Y.: Orbis, 1984.

Gutierrez, Gustavo. *A Theology of Liberation.* Rev. ed. Translated by C. Inda and J. Eagleson. Maryknoll, N.Y.: Orbis, 1988.

*Hauerwas, Stanley, and Jones, Gregory. *Why Narrative? Readings in Narrative Theology.* Grand Rapids, Mich.: Eerdmans, 1989.

Lewis, C. S. *Mere Christianity.* New York: Macmillan, 1981.

Malony, H. Newton, ed. *Current Perspectives in the Psychology of Religion.* Grand Rapids, Mich.: Eerdmans, 1977.

*Olthuis, James H., et al. *A Hermeneutics of Ultimacy.* Lanham, Md.: University Press of America, 1986.

Neill, Stephen. *Christian Faith and Other Faiths.* 3d ed. Downers Grove, Ill.: InterVarsity Press, 1984.

Niebuhr, H. Richard. *Christ and Culture.* New York: Harper & Row, 1951.

Pinnock, Clark. *The Scripture Principle.* San Francisco: Harper & Row, 1985.

Ramm, Bernard. *Varieties of Christian Apologetics.* Grand Rapids, Mich.: Baker Book House, 1974.

Thiselton, Anthony. *The Two Horizons: New Testament Hermeneutics and Philosophical Description with Special Reference to Heidegger, Bultmann, Gadamer, and Wittgenstein.* Grand Rapids, Mich.: Eerdmans, 1980.

van Huystein, Wentzel. *Theology and the Justification of Faith: Constructing Theories in Systematic Theology.* Translated by H. F. Snijders. Grand Rapids, Mich.: Eerdmans, 1989.

Further Resources:
Crux

Regent College
2130 Wesbrook Mall
Vancouver, British Columbia V6T 1W6
Canada

The Evangelical Quarterly
The Paternoster Press
3 Mount Radford Crescent
Exeter EX2 4JW
United Kingdom

Interpretation—A Journal of Bible and Theology
Union Theological Seminary
3401 Brook Rd.
Richmond, VA 23227

Themelios
IFES—Link
6400 Schroeder Road
Box 7895
Madison, WI 53707-7895

Ethics

Hauerwas, Stanley. *The Peaceable Kingdom: A Primer in Christian Ethics.* Notre
Dame, Ind.: Univ. of Notre Dame Press, 1983.

Holmes, Arthur. *Ethics: Approaching Moral Decisions.* Downers Grove, Ill.: InterVarsity Press, 1984.

*Jones, D. Gareth. *Brave New People: Ethical Issues at the Commencement of Life.*
Grand Rapids, Mich.: Eerdmans, 1985.

Longenecker, Richard N. *New Testament Social Ethics for Today.* Grand Rapids,
Mich.: Eerdmans, 1984.

MacIntyre, Alasdair. *After Virtue.* 2d ed. Notre Dame, Ind.: Univ. of Notre
Dame Press, 1984.

O'Donovan, Oliver. *Resurrection and Moral Order: An Outline for Evangelical
Ethics.* Grand Rapids, Mich.: Eerdmans, 1986.

Olthuis, James H. *I Pledge You My Troth.* 2d ed. San Francisco: Harper & Row,
1989.

*Sider, Ronald J. *Completely Pro-Life.* Downers Grove, Ill.: InterVarsity Press,

1987.

*Smedes, Lewis B. *Choices: Making Right Decisions in a Complex World.* San Francisco: Harper & Row, 1986.

_____ . *Mere Morality.* Grand Rapids, Mich.: Eerdmans, 1983.

_____ . *Sex For Christians.* Grand Rapids, Mich.: Eerdmans, 1976.

Verhey, Allen. *The Great Reversal: Ethics and the New Testament.* Grand Rapids, Mich.: Eerdmans, 1984.

Whitehead, Evelyn, and Whitehead, James. *Christian Life Patterns.* Garden City: Doubleday, 1979.

*Wright, Christopher. *An Eye for an Eye: The Place of Old Testament Ethics Today.* Downers Grove, Ill.: InterVarsity Press, 1983.

History

*Bebbington, D. W. *Patterns in History.* Downers Grove, Ill.: InterVarsity Press, 1980.

Butterfield, Herbert. *Man on His Past: The Study of the History of Historical Scholarship.* Cambridge: Cambridge University Press, 1969.

_____ . *Writings on Christianity and History.* Edited by C. T. McIntire. New York: Oxford, 1979.

Gilkey, Langdon. *Reaping the Whirlwind: A Christian Interpretation of History.* New York: Seabury, 1977.

Marsden, George, and Roberts, Frank, eds. *A Christian View of History?* Grand Rapids, Mich.: Eerdmans, 1975.

*McIntire, C. T., ed. *God, History and Historians.* New York: Oxford, 1977.

McIntire, C. T., and Wells, Ron, eds. *History and Historical Understanding.* Grand Rapids, Mich.: Eerdmans, 1984.

Niebuhr, Reinhold. *Faith and History: A Comparison of Christian and Modern Views of History.* New York: Scribner's, 1949.

*Wells, Ron. *History through the Eyes of Faith.* San Francisco: Harper & Row, 1989.

Further Resources:

Fides et Historia
Journal of the Conference on Faith and History
c/o Richard Pierard
Department of History
Indiana State University
Terre Haute, IN 47809

Psychology

Benner, David, ed. *Baker Encyclopedia of Psychology*. Grand Rapids, Mich.: Baker, 1985.

Benner, David. *Psychotherapy in Christian Perspective*. Grand Rapids, Mich.: Baker, 1987.

DeGraaff, Arnold. "Psychology: Sensitive Openness and Appropriate Reactions." Toronto: Institute for Christian Studies Academic Paper Series, n.d.

*Evans, C. Stephen. *Wisdom and Humanness in Psychology: Prospects for a Christian Approach*. Grand Rapids, Mich.: Baker, 1989.

Jones, Stanton L., ed. *Psychology and the Christian Faith: An Introductory Reader*. Grand Rapids, Mich.: Baker, 1986.

Malony, H. Newton, ed. *Wholeness and Holiness: Readings in the Psychology/Theology of Mental Health*. Grand Rapids, Mich.: Baker, 1983.

*Myers, David. *The Human Puzzle: Psychological Research and Christian Belief*. New York: Harper & Row, 1978.

*Myers, David, and Jeeves, Malcolm. *Psychology through the Eyes of Faith*. San Francisco: Harper & Row, 1989.

Tournier, Paul. *The Meaning of Persons*. New York: Harper & Row, 1982.

Van Leeuwen, Mary Stewart. *The Person in Psychology*. Grand Rapids, Mich.: Eerdmans, 1985.

*————. *The Sorcerer's Apprentice: A Christian Looks at the Changing Face of Psychology*. Downers Grove, Ill.: InterVarsity Press, 1983.

Further Resources:

Journal of Psychology and Christianity
Journal of the Christian Association for Psychological Studies
P.O. Box 628
Blue Jay, CA 92317

Journal of Psychology and Theology
Rosemead School of Theology
Biola University
13800 Biola Ave.
La Mirada, CA 90639

Sociology

Anderson, Ray, and Guernsey, Dennis. *On Being a Family: A Social Theory of the Family*. Grand Rapids, Mich.: Eerdmans, 1986.

De Santo, C. *Christian Perspectives on Social Problems*. Scottdale, Pa.: Herald Press, 1983.

*De Santo, C.; Smith-Hinds, W.; and Redekop, C. *A Reader in Sociology: Christian Perspectives*. Scottdale, Pa.: Herald Press, 1980.

Goudzwaard, Bob. *Aid for the Overdeveloped West*. Toronto: Wedge, 1975.

Grunlan, Stephen, and Reimer, M., eds. *Christian Perspective on Sociology*. Grand Rapids, Mich.: Zondervan, 1982.

Lyon, David. *Sociology and the Human Image*. Downers Grove, Ill.: InterVarsity Press, 1983.

Perkins, Richard. *Looking Both Ways: Exploring the Interface between Christianity and Sociology*. Grand Rapids, Mich.: Baker, 1987.

Storkey, Alan. *A Christian Social Perspective*. Leicester, U.K.: Inter-Varsity Press, 1979.

Further Resources:
National Association for Christians in Social Work
P.O. Box 90
St. Davids, PA 19087

Sociology and Christianity: An Annotated Bibliography
Compiled by: The Ilkey Group
Leicester, U.K.: UCCF Associates, 1979

Note: People in sociology and social work should also pay attention to the resources listed under "Psychology," "Political Studies," and "Economics and Commerce."

Economics and Commerce
Clouse, Robert, ed. *Wealth and Poverty: Four Christian Views of Economics*. Downers Grove, Ill.: InterVarsity Press, 1984.

Cramp, A. B. *Notes toward a Christian Critique of Secular Economic Theory*. Toronto: Institute for Christian Studies, 1975.

Ellul, Jacques. *Money and Power*. Translated by LaVonne Neff. Downers Grove, Ill.: InterVarsity Press, 1984.

*Goudzwaard, Bob. *Capitalism and Progress: A Diagnosis of Western Society*. Translated by Josina Van Nuis Zylstra. Grand Rapids, Mich.: Eerdmans, 1979.

Griffiths, Brian. *The Creation of Wealth*. Downers Grove, Ill.: InterVarsity Press,

1984.

Justice in the International Economic Order. Proceedings of the 2d Conference for Christian Higher Education. Grand Rapids, Mich.: Calvin College, 1980.

Owensby, Walter. *Economics for Prophets: A Primer on Concepts, Realities and Values in Our Economic System.* Grand Rapids, Mich.: Eerdmans, 1989.

Richardson, J. David. "Frontiers in Economics and Christian Scholarship." *Christian Scholar's Review* 17, 4 (June 1988):381-400. (Includes a comprehensive bibliography.)

Schumacher, E. F. *Small Is Beautiful: Economics as if People Mattered.* New York: Harper & Row, 1976.

*Sider, Ronald J. *Rich Christians in an Age of Hunger: A Biblical Study.* 2d ed. Downers Grove, Ill.: InterVarsity Press, 1984.

Stackhouse, Max. *Public Theology and Political Economy: Christian Stewardship in Modern Society.* Grand Rapids, Mich.: Eerdmans, 1987.

*Storkey, Alan. *Transforming Economics: A Christian Way to Employment.* London: SPCK, 1986.

Ward, Benjamin. *The Ideal Worlds of Economics: Liberal, Radical and Conservative Economic World Views.* New York: Basic Books, 1979.

Wogoman, John Philip. *The Great Economic Debate: An Ethical Analysis.* Philadelphia: Westminster, 1977.

Note: People in economics and commerce should also pay attention to the resources listed under "Sociology" and "Political Studies," and those listed in section IV, "After School: Work and Leisure."

Political Studies

Changing Course: A Study for Canadian Social Analysis. Toronto: Citizens for Public Justice, 1987. (For address, see "Further Resources" below.)

Ellul, Jacques. *The Politics of God and the Politics of Man.* Grand Rapids, Mich.: Eerdmans, 1972.

Fowler, Robert Booth. *A New Engagement: Evangelical Political Thought, 1966-1976.* Grand Rapids, Mich.: Eerdmans, 1982.

Goudzwaard, Bob. *A Christian Political Option.* Toronto: Wedge, 1972.

*Malloch, Ted, and Harper, William A., eds. *Where Are We Now? The State of Christian Political Reflection.* Lanham, Md.: University Press of America, 1981.

*Marshall, Paul. *Thine Is the Kingdom: A Biblical Perspective on Government and

Politics Today. Grand Rapids, Mich.: Eerdmans, 1984.

Monsma, Stephen V. *Pursuing Justice in a Sinful World.* Grand Rapids, Mich.: Eerdmans, 1984.

Mott, Stephen C. *Biblical Ethics and Social Change.* New York: Oxford, 1982.

Mouw, Richard J. *Politics and the Biblical Drama.* Grand Rapids, Mich.: Baker, 1983.

Neuhaus, Richard John. *The Naked Public Square: Religion and Democracy in America.* Grand Rapids, Mich.: Eerdmans, 1984.

Sider, Ronald J. *Cry Justice: The Bible on Poverty and Hunger.* Ramsey, N.J.: Paulist Press; Downers Grove, Ill.: InterVarsity Press, 1980.

Sider, Ronald J., ed. *Evangelicals and Development: Toward a Theology of Social Change.* Philadelphia: Westminster, 1982.

Simon, Arthur. *Christian Faith and Public Policy: No Grounds for Divorce.* Grand Rapids, Mich.: Eerdmans, 1987.

*Spykman, Gordon, et al. *Let My People Live: Faith and Struggle in Central America.* Grand Rapids, Mich.: Eerdmans, 1988.

Villa-Vicencio, Charles, ed. *Theology and Violence: The South African Debate.* Grand Rapids, Mich.: Eerdmans, 1988.

Wolterstorff, Nicholas. *Until Justice and Peace Embrace.* Grand Rapids, Mich.: Eerdmans, 1984.

Yoder, John Howard. *The Politics of Jesus.* Grand Rapids, Mich.: Eerdmans, 1972.

Further Resources:
Public Justice Report
Periodical of the Association for Public Justice
806 15th St. NW
Suite 440
Washington, DC 20005

Catalyst
Periodical of Citizens for Public Justice
229 College St.
Toronto, Ontario M5T 1R4

Note: Students in political studies should also pay attention to resources listed under "Sociology" and "Economics."

The following journals are helpful for people in sociology, political studies and economics. They also frequently publish articles on the arts, popular culture, contemporary media and various other disciplines.

Sojourners
1398 L. St. NW
Washington, DC 20005

The Other Side
300 Apsley St.
Philadelphia, PA 19144

Reformed Journal
255 Jefferson Ave SE
Grand Rapids, MI 49503

Christian Scholar's Review
c/o Calvin College
Grand Rapids, MI 49506

Radix
P.O. Box 4307
Berkeley, CA 94702

Art and Aesthetics
Apostolos-Cappadona, Diane, ed. *Art, Creativity and the Sacred.* New York: Crossroad, 1985.
Deart, Tim, and Porter, David, eds. *Art in Question.* London Lectures in Contemporary Christianity. London: Marshall Pickering, 1982.
Edgar, William. *Taking Note of Music.* London: SPCK, 1986.
*Forbes, Cheryl. *Imagination: Embracing a Theology of Wonder.* Portland, Ore.: Multnomah Press, 1986.
Lockerbie, D. Bruce, ed. *The Timeless Moment: Creativity and the Christian Faith.* Westchester, Ill.: Cornerstone, 1981.
Rookmaaker, Hans. *The Creative Gift: Essays on Art and Christian Life.* Westchester, Ill.: Good News, 1981.
———. *Modern Art and the Death of a Culture.* Downers Grove, Ill.: InterVarsity Press, 1970.

Ryken, Leland, ed. *The Christian Imagination.* Grand Rapids, Mich.: Baker, 1981.

Ryken, Leland. *Culture in Christian Perspective: A Door to Understanding and Enjoying the Arts.* Portland, Ore.: Multnomah Press, 1986.

*Seerveld, Calvin G. *Rainbows for the Fallen World.* Toronto: Tuppance Press; Beaver Falls, Pa.: Radix Books, 1980.

Vos, Nelvin. *The Great Pendulum of Becoming: Images in Modern Drama.* Grand Rapids, Mich.: Eerdmans, 1981.

*Wilson, John. *One of the Richest Gifts: An Introductory Study of the Arts from a Christian Worldview.* Edinburgh: The Handsel Press, 1981.

*Wolterstorff, Nicholas. *Art in Action.* Grand Rapids, Mich.: Eerdmans, 1980.

_____ . *Works and Worlds of Art.* New York: Oxford University Press, 1980.

Media Studies and Communications

Bachman, John W. *Media—Wasteland or Wonderland: Opportunities and Dangers for Christians in the Electronic Age.* Minneapolis: Augsburg, 1984.

Christians, Clifford G. "A Cultural View of Mass Communications: Some Explorations for Christians." *Christian Scholar's Review* 7,1 (1977):3-22.

Ellul, Jacques. *The Humiliation of the Word.* Grand Rapids, Mich.: Eerdmans, 1985.

Fore, W. F. *Television and Religion: The Shaping of Faith, Values and Culture.* Minneapolis: Augsburg, 1987.

Goethals, Gregor. *The TV Ritual: Worship at the Video Altar.* Boston: Beacon Press, 1981.

*Greeley, Andrew M. *God in Popular Culture.* Chicago: Thomas More Press, 1988.

Horsfield, Peter. *Religious Television.* New York: Longman, 1984.

*Lyon, David. *The Information Society.* New York: Basil Blackwell, 1988.

Owens, Virginia Stem. *The Total Image: On Selling Jesus in the Modern Age.* Grand Rapids, Mich.: Eerdmans, 1980.

*Nelson, John W. *Your God Is Alive and Well and Appearing in Popular Culture.* Philadelphia: Westminster, 1976.

Postman, Neil. *Amusing Ourselves to Death.* New York: Penguin, 1985.

Schultze, Quentin. *Television: Manna from Hollywood.* Grand Rapids, Mich.: Zondervan, 1986.

Literature

Berry, Wendell. *Standing by Words.* St. Louis, Mo.: North Point, 1983.

Dillard, Annie. *Living by Fiction.* San Francisco: Harper & Row, 1982.

Ericson, E. E., Jr., and Tennyson, G. B., eds. *Religion and Modern Literature: Essays in Theory and Criticism.* Grand Rapids, Mich.: Eerdmans, 1975.

Ficken, Carl. *God's Story and Modern Literature: Reading Fiction in Community.* Philadelphia: Fortress, 1985.

Lewis, C. S. *Studies in Words.* Cambridge: Cambridge University Press, 1974.

*Lundin, Roger, and Gallagher, Susan. *Literature through the Eyes of Faith.* San Francisco: Harper & Row, 1989.

*Ryken, Leland. *Triumphs of the Imagination.* Downers Grove, Ill.: InterVarsity Press, 1979.

Ryken, Leland, ed. *The Christian Imagination: Essays on Literature and the Arts.* Grand Rapids, Mich.: Baker, 1981.

Sire, James W. *How to Read Slowly.* Wheaton, Ill.: Harold Shaw, 1989.

TeSelle, S. F. *Literature and the Christian Life.* New Haven: Yale University Press, 1966.

Timmerman, John, and Hettinga, Donald. *In the World: Reading and Writing as a Christian.* Grand Rapids, Mich.: Baker, 1987.

Tischler, Nancy. *A Voice of Her Own: Women, Literature and Transformation.* Grand Rapids, Mich.: Zondervan, 1987.

Further Resources:

Christianity and Literature: An Interdisciplinary Journal
Journal of the Conference on Christianity and Literature
c/o English Department
Baylor University
Waco, TX 76798-7404

Note: People in music would find assistance in some of the books listed under "Art and Aesthetics," "Media Studies and Communications," and "Literature."

Women's Studies

Bilezikian, Gilbert. *Beyond Sex Roles: A Guide for the Study of Female Roles in the Bible.* Grand Rapids, Mich.: Baker, 1985.

Clouse, Bonnidell, and Clouse, Robert G. *Women in Ministry: Four Views.* Downers Grove, Ill.: InterVarsity Press, 1989. (Includes an excellent bibliography.)

*Evans, Mary J. *Woman in the Bible.* Downers Grove, Ill.: InterVarsity Press; Exeter: Paternoster, 1983.

Hagan, June S., ed. *Gender Matters: Women's Studies for the Christian Community*. Grand Rapids, Mich.: Zondervan, 1989.

Mickelsen, Alvera, ed. *Women, Authority and the Bible*. Downers Grove, Ill.: InterVarsity Press, 1986.

Mollenkott, Virginia Ramey. *The Divine Feminine: The Biblical Language of the God as Female*. New York: Crossroad, 1983.

Scanzoni, Letha, and Hardesty, Nancy. *All We're Meant to Be: Biblical Feminism for Today*. Waco, Tex.: Word, 1974.

Sneiders, Sandra. *Women and the Word: The Gender of God in the New Testament and the Spirituality of Women*. New York: Paulist Press, 1986.

*Storkey, Elaine. *What's Right with Feminism*. London: SPCK, 1985; and Grand Rapids, Mich.: Eerdmans, 1986.

Trible, Phyllis. *God and the Rhetoric of Sexuality*. Philadelphia: Fortress, 1978.

*Van Leeuwen, Mary Stewart. *Gender and Grace*. Downers Grove, Ill.: InterVarsity Press, 1990.

Education

Brueggeman, Walter. *The Creative Word: Canon as a Model for Biblical Education*. Philadelphia: Fortress, 1982.

Freire, P. *Pedagogy of the Oppressed*. New York: Continuum, 1970.

*Groome, Thomas. *Christian Religious Education*. New York: Harper & Row, 1980.

Harris, Maria. *Teaching and Religious Imagination*. San Francisco: Harper & Row, 1987.

Hill, Brian V. *Faith at the Blackboard: Issues Facing The Christian Teacher*. Grand Rapids, Mich.: Eerdmans, 1982.

Holmes, Arthur. *The Idea of a Christian College*. Grand Rapids, Mich.: Eerdmans, 1975.

McCarthy, Rockne, et al. *Society, State and Schools: A Case for Structural and Confessional Pluralism*. Grand Rapids, Mich.: Eerdmans, 1981.

Mechielsen, Jack. *No Icing on the Cake*. Melbourne: Brookes-Hall Publishing, 1980.

Miller, Donald E. *Story and Context: An Introduction to Christian Education*. Nashville: Abingdon, 1987.

Pazmiño, Robert. *Foundational Issues in Christian Education*. Grand Rapids, Mich.: Baker, 1988.

*Peterson, Michael L. *Philosophy of Education: Issues and Options*. Downers Grove, Ill.: InterVarsity Press, 1986.

Purpel, David E. *The Moral and Spiritual Crisis in Education.* Granby, Mass.: Bergin and Garvey, 1989.

Roques, Mark. *Curriculum Unmasked: Towards a Christian Understanding of Education.* London: Monarch, 1989.

Steensma, Geraldine, and Van Brummelen, Harro, eds. *Shaping School Curriculum: A Biblical View.* Terre Haute, Ind.: Signal Press, 1977.

*Van Brummelen, Harro. *Walking with God in the Classroom.* Burlington, Ont.: Welch Publishing, 1988.

Wolterstorff, Nicholas. *Educating for Responsible Action.* Grand Rapids, Mich.: Eerdmans, 1982.

Law and Criminology

*Berman, Harold. *Law and Revolution: The Formation of the Western Legal Tradition.* Boston: Harvard University Press, 1985.

Marshall, Paul. *Human Rights Theories in Christian Perspective.* Toronto: Institute for Christian Studies, 1983.

Smarto, Donald A. *Justice and Mercy: A Christian Solution to America's Correctional Crisis.* Wheaton, Ill.: Tyndale House, 1987.

Stackhouse, Max. *Creeds, Society and Human Rights: A Study of Three Cultures.* Grand Rapids, Mich.: Eerdmans, 1984.

*Stott, John, and Miller, Nick, eds. *Crime and the Responsible Community.* Grand Rapids, Mich.: Eerdmans, 1980.

Umbreit, Mark. *Crime and Reconciliation: Creative Options for Victims and Offenders.* Nashville: Abingdon, 1985.

Van Ness, Daniel. *Crime and its Victims.* Downers Grove, Ill.: InterVarsity Press, 1986.

*Witte, John, ed. *The Weightier Matters of the Law: Essays on Law and Religion.* Decatur, Ga.: Scholars Press, 1988.

IV. After School: Work and Leisure

Diehl, William. *Thank God It's Monday.* Philadelphia: Fortress, 1982.

Frey, Bradshaw, et al. *At Work, At Play: Biblical Insight for Daily Obedience.* Jordan Station, Ont.: Paideia Press, 1986.

*Marshall, Paul, et al. *Labour of Love: Essays on Work.* Toronto: Wedge, 1980.

Pountney, Michael. *Getting a Job: A Guide for Choosing a Career.* Downers Grove, Ill.: InterVarsity Press, 1984.

*Redekop, Calvin, and Bender, Urie A. *Who Am I? What Am I?—Searching for Meaning in Your Work.* Grand Rapids, Mich.: Zondervan, 1988.

Ryken, Leland. *Work and Leisure in Christian Perspective.* Portland, Ore.: Multnomah Press, 1987.

Shelly, Judith Allen. *Not Just a Job: Serving Christ in Your Work.* Downers Grove, Ill.: InterVarsity Press, 1985.

*Tucker, Graham. *The Faith-Work Connection: A Practical Application of Christian Values in the Marketplace.* Toronto: Anglican Book Centre, 1987.

Subject Index

Adams, Douglas, *203*
Adler, Mortimer, *214*
Allen, David E., *227*
Alter, Robert, *173, 215*
Anderson, Bernhard W., *230*
Anderson, Ray, *234*
Animism, *45*
Apostolos-Cappadona, Diane, *238*
Arnold, Matthew, *174, 216*
Austin, Richard Cartwright, *224*
Bachman, John W., *239*
Bacon, Francis, *132*
Baker, T., *225*
Barbour, Ian, *223*
Barclay, William, *91, 201, 208*
Barrett, William, *222*
Barrs, Jerram, *202*
Barth, Karl, *206*
Bartusiak, Marcia, *203*
Basho, Matsuo, *170-72, 215*
Baudelaire, Charles, *183, 216*
Bauma, Hessel, *227*
Bebbington, D. W., *233*
Bellah, Robert, *58, 62-63, 202, 206, 222*
Bellow, Saul, *158*
Benner, David, *233*
Berger, Peter, *220, 222*
Berkhof, Hendrikus, *231*
Berman, Harold, *242*

Berry, Wendell, *211, 227, 239*
Bilezikian, Gilbert, *240*
Bird, Lewis P., *227*
Black, McKnight, *131*
Blackham, H. J., *216*
Blamires, Harry, *12, 198, 201, 220*
Blomberg, Craig, *230*
Bloom, Allan, *208-9, 214-15*
Board, C. Stephen, *208*
Boesak, Alan, *231*
Bolter, J. David, *210, 226*
Borg, Marcus, *230*
Boswell, James, *206*
Bouma, Hessel, *227*
Brabenac, R. L., *226*
Bromiley, Geoffrey, *42, 204*
Brown, Colin, *205, 207, 229*
Brown, Raymond, *207*
Brueggemann, Walter, *220, 224, 230, 241*
Buddhism, *45*
Burke, Thomas J., *213*
Butterfield, Herbert, *233*
Calvin, John, *94, 147, 208, 212-13*
Calvin Center for Christian Scholarship, *122, 127-28, 131, 134-36, 210-11*
Camus, Albert, *158, 164, 209*
Carmody, John, *225*
Carpenter, Joel, *221*
Casserly, Langmead, *229*

Chan, Wing-tsit, *81, 206-7*
Chase, Gene B., *226*
Childs, Brevard, *230*
Christians, Clifford G., *239*
Chuang Chou, *78, 80, 83, 95, 206, 116, 209*
Clouse, Robert, *235, 240*
Coleman, Bruce, *227*
Collins, Joseph, *228*
Comte, Auguste, *145-46*
Conrad, Joseph, *164-65, 171, 214*
Conyers, A. J., *209*
Copernicus, *144*
Cosgrove, Mark, *213*
Coyne, G. V., *225*
Craigie, Peter, *184-85, 216*
Cramp, A. B., *235*
Crane, Stephen, *158*
Culler, Jonathan, *173, 215*
Cultural mandate, *67-69*
Darwin, Charles, *144*
Deart, Tim, *238*
Debrunner, A., *207*
DeGraff, Arnold, *234*
DeSanto, C., *234*
Descartes, *18*
Diehl, William *242*
Dillard, Annie, *13, 160, 187, 201, 214, 216-17, 239*
Dodd, C. H., *207*
Dooyeweerd, Herman, *222, 229*
Dreyfus, Hubert L., *226*
Dreyfus, Stuart E., *226*
Dykema, Eugene R., *134*
Edgar, William, *238*

Scanzoni, Letha, *241*
Schaeffer, Francis A., *209, 211, 225*
Schouls, Peter A., *229*
Schultze, Quentin, *239*
Schumacher, E. F., *158, 226, 236*
Schuurman, Egbert, *134, 227*
Seerveld, Calvin, *229-30, 239*
Shakespeare, William, *76, 206*
Shelly, Judith Allen, *227, 242*
Shelly, Mary, *132-33, 211*
Shipps, Kenneth W., *221*
Sider, Ronald J., *232, 236-37*
Simon, Arthur, *228, 237*
Sinnema, Donald, *221*
Sire, James W., *29-30, 41, 165, 202, 204, 214-16, 220-21*
Skinner, B. F., *151-55, 157-58, 198, 213-14*
Slade, Alan, *210*
Smart, Ninian, *220*
Smarto, Donald A., *242*
Smedes, Lewis B., *232*
Smith-Hinds, W., *234*
Sneiders, Sandra, *241*
Snyder, Gary, *42, 164, 206*
Sproul, R. C., *209*
Spykman, Gordon, *237*
Stackhouse, Max, *236, 242*
Stafleu, Marinus Dirk, *223, 225*
Steensma, Geraldine, *226, 241*
Sterrett, Norton, *209*
Stevenson, Leslie, *220*
Stoeger, W. R., *225*
Storkey, Alan A., *235-36, 241*
Stott, John R. W., *22, 202, 211, 221, 242*
Swartley, Willard, *230*

Technicism, *132*
Technology, *119-38*
Templeton, John, *223*
Tennyson, G. B., *239*
Tennyson, Lord Alfred, *22, 202*
TeSelle, S. F., *240*
Theism, *39, 47-50, 117, 147*
Theissen, Gerd, *230*
Thiselton, Anthony, *231*
Thomas, Lewis, *46, 73, 205-6*
Thurman, Duane, *212*
Timmerman, John, *240*
Tischler, Nancy A., *240*
Tocqueville, Alexis de, *206*
Toffler, Alvin, *28, 202*
Tournier, Paul, *234*
Tribble, Phyllis, *241*
Tucker, Graham, *242*
Turkle, Sherry, *210*
Uedo, Makoto, *215*
Umbreit, Mark, *242*
Underwager, Ralph C., *214*
Upanishads, *45*
Vander Goot, Mary, *213*
Vander Vennen, Robert, *228*
Van Brummelen, Harro, *226, 241-42*
van Huystein, Wentzel, *231*
Van Leeuwen, Mary, *146, 151, 213, 229, 234, 241*
Van Ness, *242*
Van Poolen, Lambert J., *134*
Van Till, Howard, *223-25*
Vaux, Kenneth, *227*
Verhey, Allen, *227, 233*
Vieth, Gene Edward, Jr., *198, 221*
Villa-Vincencio, Charles, *237*
Vitz, Paul, *146, 213*
Voran, Marilyn Helmuth,

228
Vos, Nelvin, *239*
Walhout, Clarence, *173-74, 216*
Wallis, Jim, *221*
Walsh, Brian, *122, 198, 210, 219-42, 220, 222*
Walter, Tony, *202, 222*
Ward, Benjamin, *236*
Watson, J. B., *145-46*
Weisel, Elie, *164*
Wells, David, *221*
Wells, Ron, *233*
Westminster Confession, *41, 68, 204*
White, Lynn, Jr., *211*
Whitehead, Alfred, *32, 203, 212*
Whitehead, Evelyn, *233*
Whitehead, James, *233*
Whitman, Walt, *62-63*
Wiester, John, *224*
Wilkes, Peter, *221*
Wilkinson, Loren, *225*
Wilson, John, *239*
Winner, Langdon, *123, 128-29, 210, 227*
Witte, John, *242*
Wogoman, John Philip, *236*
Wolfe, David L., *209, 221, 229*
Wolters, Albert, *221, 229*
Wolterstroff, Nicholas, *211, 222, 229, 237, 239, 242*
Wordsworth, William, *13, 16-17, 42, 201*
Wright, Christopher, *231, 233*
Wright, Richard T., *224*
Wright, Tom, *230*
Yandell, Keith, *229*
Yeats, William Butler, *173, 215*
Yoder, John Howard, *19, 191, 202-3, 217, 237*
Yoder, Perry, *231*
Zen, *164, 171-72, 215*

Scripture Index